MISSIONARY MESSAGES

Missionary Messages

A. B. SIMPSON

CHRISTIAN PUBLICATIONS

CAMP HILL, PENNSYLVANIA

Christian Publications
3825 Hartzdale Drive, Camp Hill, PA 17011

The mark of ✝ vibrant faith

ISBN: 0-87509-397-3
LOC Catalog Card Number: 87-71136
© 1987 by Christian Publications
All rights reserved
Printed in the United States of America
Cover photo by Mike Saunier

CONTENTS

INTRODUCTION

ALBERT B. SIMPSON, FOUNDER of The Christian and Missionary Alliance, has been widely recognized as one of the foremost missionary leaders of the century. His messages were used of God to move the church of the Lord Jesus Christ to a new sense of accountability for the neglected people of the world. He was an advocate for the lost before the conscience of North America.

When pleading for foreign missions, Simpson's consecrated powers of expression by tongue and pen were at their best. Multiplied thousands had the privilege of hearing him. Many of them were won to a partnership in the missionary cause through his burning words. This treasured collection of his stirring addresses will give the reader something of the hallowed memories surrounding the Old Orchard Beach conferences in Maine and his Gospel Tabernacle in New York City. They will strengthen the faith of those who have cherished the missionary vision through the years.

The worldwide movement that Simpson initiated is still going forward with ever-increasing momentum. He built wisely, with Christ rather than himself in the foreground. When his personal leadership was no longer available, the teachings and principles that he enunciated continued to hold his followers together in loyalty to his great objectives. Some of the secrets of this permanent building will be found in these messages. All who would become missionaries of the cross or sharers by prayer and sacrifice in the world's noblest enterprise will do well to study them carefully.

The chief purpose in sending forth this volume is to pass along the inspiration of these words of truth to a new generation. May a multitude of lives be offered unto God for His glorious service through these messages. And may many of God's stewards be quickened to a greater sense of their privilege and responsibility!

W.M. Turnbull
1925

This 1988 reissue of Missionary Messages *comes as the church Albert B. Simpson founded enters its second century of world ministry. And the burden the author shares is just as pertinent today as the day he wrote it.*

May these messages, carefully reedited in updated language, be used of God to motivate still other generations and thus hasten Christ's certain return.

The Editors

The Missionary Emergency

A N EMERGENCY IS A SITUATION of such extreme need that responsibility must not be delayed. It is a case of life or death, now or never. Envision a hundred entombed miners signaling from the depths of some exploded coal shaft. Rescuers are racing to the mouth of the mine for instant relief. The miners' wives and children are sobbing, their hearts crushed in dismay. That is an emergency.

When on the white fields of the Northwest the great harvest is perishing for lack of laborers, and almost any price is offered for men to save the crops that must either be reaped or rot, that is an emergency. When the signal flares are flashing over some raging surf, revealing terrified men clinging to the sides of a vessel floundering in the angry sea, that is an emergency.

When the call for reinforcements comes from a military unit, hard pressed by outnumbering foes, struggling to hold a strategic point, that is an emergency. When the sirens scream at the midnight hour and lurid flames are bursting from roof and windows of a residence, that is an emergency.

Who would dare to blame those who spring to the

rescue for their enthusiasm? Who would dare call them mad? Their names are honored as the heroes of their country, and the stories of their sacrifice light up our history with a glorious brilliance.

There are spiritual emergencies

But there are greater crises and mightier emergencies in the higher world of our spiritual work and warfare. One of these is the great task of working and praying and sacrificing for the immediate evangelization of the world. This is not merely a duty. It is the supreme task of every Christian. This is not merely a question of Christian privilege. It is a Christian obligation. It is not merely an opportunity. It is an emergency. The true servant of God is "redeeming the time"—buying up the opportunity—"because the days are evil" (Ephesians 5:16).

It is an emergency because of lost humanity's awful need. This is no mere question of temporal, material or local interest. It is a question of eternal destiny, of eternal life or death. Concerning this question, the Master Himself has said, "What shall it profit a man, if he shall gain the whole world, and lose his own soul?" (Mark 8:36). Compared with this tremendous issue, the ordinary questions of sanitation, civic reform, municipal government, tax legislation, national prosperity, social reform—even of war and peace—are trivial. The work of world missions is imperative!

It is an emergency because the need is so vast. Were all the human family to march past, rank on rank, and hear the gospel only once, the procession would take a lifetime. Over those perishing multitudes, the heart of the Master yearns with infinite compassion as He cries out from age to age, "The harvest truly is plenteous, but the labourers are few" (Matthew 9:37). What question can compare with the question of their need and of our responsibility?

We have no time to lose

It is an emergency because these multitudes are swiftly passing beyond our reach. The Christless world of which we speak, while it is ever present in its mass, is ever passing in its individual members. If we are ever to save our generation, it must be now.

It is an emergency because of the awful spiritual destitution of the world that knows not Jesus, and the disproportion of its opportunity to hear of Him. There are vast millions of people overseas who are virtually devoid of any gospel witness, while in America we have scores of churches in almost every city. Is this fair? Is this loyalty to the Master? Is this being honest to our trust? Or is this a breach of trust, treason against our Lord and bloodguiltiness for the souls of men and women?

It is an emergency because of the continual growth in world population. In spite of the rapid progress of missionary ministries overseas, the rate of population increase far exceeds the number of people being reached for Christ.

It is an emergency because the leaders of false religions and false cults have increased their activity. The very excitement of missions has stimulated our adversary to imitate the missionary crusade. On every hand there is a reaction to Christian missions and a revival of evil forces. This activity calls for the most strenuous emergency work on the part of the followers of the Lord.

The extraordinary openings God has brought

about recently in some lands create an unequaled opportunity and a real emergency. God has answered the prayers of our fathers to remove the barriers and to open doors. Not only are the doors open, but they are off the hinges and the walls are down! Our God is marching through every land, opening the way for the entrance of the gospel.

All of this is enhanced by the equally wonderful working of the Holy Spirit in the hearts of men and women as the gospel is preached to them. It is an age of marvelous ingathering. From nation after nation comes word of multiplied spiritual conversions. The labors of the foreign missionary are resulting in a large harvest. If we would invest our lives and our money where God is working most effectively and marvelously, we would all be missionaries.

A crisis as well as a call

What an opportunity! What an emergency! But it is a crisis as well as a call. The open doors may suddenly close. Paul said of the city of Ephesus, "A great door and effectual is opened unto me, and there are many adversaries" (1 Corinthians 16:9). The awakened people who are asking for spiritual bread may be cheated with a serpent and a stone. Western culture is not necessarily Christian. If we do not give people Christ, they will soon be found accepting Western culture's agnosticism and its cold materialism. The very suddenness of the reaction from the past demands immediate action on the part of the church of God. Otherwise we shall face a new closed door. Surely this is a supreme emergency.

The signs of the soon coming of the Lord Jesus intensify the crisis and the emergency. If the preaching of the gospel unto all nations as a witness is the one urgent condition that will bring the end, surely no more powerful incentive to worldwide evangelization can appeal to our hearts. At best our work is only apprentice work, preliminary and preparatory to His great finishing touch. How we long for the Master to come and bring that climax to our poor, imperfect attempts at service!

Someone tells of a gifted artist who was struggling to express on canvas the great vision that had come to his soul. At last, discouraged by his inability to do justice to his own ideal, he left the painting incomplete and wrote in his diary a little cry of self-despair. That night his old master came to the studio to which he still retained a key. As he looked at the striking outline on the canvas, he thought of the artist whose inmost soul he understood so well. He seemed to enter into his concept, and, seizing a brush, he finished the painting as only he could have done.

When the young artist returned to the studio, he gazed in rapt astonishment at his finished work. Bursting into tears, he cried, "No one but the master himself could have done this!" So some day our Master will come and finish our poor apprentice work with His own glorious touch. The things that for 20 centuries the struggling church has been inadequately endeavoring to accomplish will burst upon the vision of the universe in all the glory of His finished plan. A nation has been born in a day, and the knowledge of the Lord shall cover the earth as the waters cover the sea.

It is true that God has finished making full provision for the church. The Holy Spirit has fulfilled every need in preparation for the bride. The advent chariots are only waiting until the last tribe has heard the message and received an invitation to the marriage of the Lamb.

Surely all this creates an emergency, a responsibility, a supreme incentive sufficient to set our hearts on fire, to redeem the time and finish our great missionary trust before our generation shall have passed away.

How will we respond?

These words from Paul suggest the response of Christian faith and courage to this great responsibility. "I will tarry," the apostle says, ". . . for a great door and effectual is opened unto me, and there are many adversaries" (1 Corinthians 16:8–9). This twofold challenge of opportunity and opposition calls for immediate and courageous response. The very fact that the work was difficult awakened more intense determination on the part of the apostle to face the adversary and finish the fight.

The word *tarry* emphasizes the kind of courage and resolution the task requires. This work of God calls not for meteoric showers but for fixed stars. It calls for a brave advance, for men and women who can stand firm in faith and hopefulness in Christ through the battle and be found victorious at the end of the fight.

The battle of Waterloo was won by a Scottish regiment that held a strategic point through all that dreadful day. Again and again they asked permission to charge, but the answer came back, "Stand firm!" The courier returned to his commander with the reply, "You will find us all here." Sure enough, when the battle was over, the Scotsmen were still at their posts. Broken and bruised, their rigid fingers were still holding high their unsullied flag!

A missionary doctor in India used to tell about a horse that had a habit of shying. After many ineffectual attempts to make the animal go straight, the coachman finally resorted to an ingenious strategy. Taking a long stick with a cord on the far end, he tied the cord around one ear of the horse. When the horse would shy at some object, the driver would twist the cord just enough to take the attention of the horse away from whatever was frightening it. Actually the horse became so accustomed to the cord that at hitching-up time, he would voluntarily turn his head to get the cord wound around his ear!

We should respond on principle

The missionary doctor complained that the churches of North America never seemed ready to give to missions until they were wound up by some strong missionary appeal. Surely we who know and love the Lord ought to give on principle and make our missionary offerings as systematic as our regular devotions.

Our own work has suffered much from the failure of friends to tarry at Ephesus. Many have begun well, but they have turned aside. How sad is the trail of wreckage along the way! Lives consecrated to the mission field have been sidetracked. Stewards assuming the support of foreign workers have dropped their solemn responsibility with impunity. Only a miracle of Providence and grace has carried our missionary work through these tests and discouragements.

May God give us the courage to withstand in the evil day, and having done all, to stand. May we show the love that bears and forbears and will not tire. May God give us the faith that faints not in the hour of trial.

May we have the fidelity that can look into the Master's face and say, "You will find us faithful when You return."

The New Testament Pattern

T HROUGH THE PROPHET EZEKIEL, God gives command respecting the temple which will yet rise on
Mount Moriah from the wreckage of the millenia:

> *Shew the house to the house of Israel, . . . and let them*
> *measure the pattern. And if they be ashamed of all that*
> *they have done, shew them the form of the house, and*
> *the fashion thereof, and the goings out thereof, and the*
> *comings in thereof, and all the forms thereof, and all the*
> *ordinances thereof, and all the forms thereof, and all the*
> *laws thereof. (Ezekiel 43:10–11)*

Although spoken about an earthly temple, the words
have their deepest significance, however, in the spiritual temple of which that physical temple was but a
type. They point to the great house of God's building
that consists of ransomed people. It is a house built on
the foundation of Christ Jesus Himself.

This spiritual house has a divine pattern. Just as the
tabernacle of old was to be constructed strictly according to the pattern that was shown to Moses on
the Mount, so the spiritual church of Christ has a
divine plan. It behooves us to construct it accordingly
in every particular. Failure to do so has been the cause

of the apostasies, declensions and mistakes of the past centuries. Failure to do so is the reason so much of our world still lies in darkness, crying out to God against the unfaithfulness of God's people.

Let us look more closely at this plan as Christ Himself unfolded it. We focus especially on its relationship to world evangelization. I see 12 steps to its fulfillment.

Step 1: Survey the need

The first step in the work of world evangelization is to look intelligently at the situation. Was this not the Master's admonition? "Lift up your eyes, and look on the fields; for they are white already to harvest" (John 4:35).

An intelligent concept of the needs of the world is the foundation of all true Christian work. As a rule, however, Christians know too little about the great outlying world. And they think about it in terms of evangelization even less. How many could intelligently assess the number of yet-to-be-reached people in India, China, Peru or throughout the continent of Africa? Our own little family circle and church group absorb our interests. Those considerations are more important to us than 3 billion perishing people worldwide with little hope of hearing the gospel by which alone they can be saved.

Our vision is so limited we cannot see beyond the bounds of our own denominations. We waste millions of dollars in multiplying churches simply to spread our particular sect. We do this despite the fact that whole nations are virtually without a witness to proclaim the good news of Christ and His salvation.

The need is not only vast but immediate. "Say not

ye, There are yet four months, and then cometh harvest? behold . . . the fields . . . are white already to harvest" (John 4:35). The present generation must save the present generation. Our concern must be the present generation.

The fields are white. The doors are open. The needs are urgent. Let us understand those needs. Let us study missionary geography and missionary demography under the burning light of the Holy Spirit. Let us ask God to write on our hearts the names of people, tribes and tongues. May we not rest until we have gone to them with the message of salvation.

Step 2: Pray

The second step in the evangelization of the world is prayer. Hear Jesus' exhortation to His followers: "The harvest truly is great, but the labourers are few; pray ye therefore the Lord of the harvest, that he would send forth labourers into his harvest" (Luke 10:2).

If we look at the fields, the most hopeful of us comes from the vision utterly discouraged. The needs are staggering; the resources, so apparently lacking. True, there are gleams of encouragement. Millions of people have entered eternity with hope in their hearts. Millions more are living for Jesus here and now. But the world population increase continues to outdistance those the church is winning to Christ.

In the first century, it seemed so different. In a single generation Paul and his associates planted the gospel successfully in almost every part of the Roman Empire and beyond. How could that be? They had no machines to facilitate their efforts—no automobiles or airplanes to whisk them from one point to another.

They were backed by no well-organized missionary agency, no great missionary offerings, no printed reports of their progress. But the Almighty God was in their work. In a single missionary itinerary, Paul was able to plant the gospel in all of Greece and lay the foundations of mighty churches for the ensuing centuries!

In our own day we have seen touches of God's mighty power. They are examples of what God can do and will do if we let Him.

And how does this come about? By the ministry of prayer. The world is to be evangelized by a church on her knees. This is God's work; we are to recognize Him in it. When God's supernatural touch is fully realized, nations will be born in a day. It happens when we pray. Therefore, let us pray!

Step 3: Send selected workers

The New Testament plan of missions involved the sending out of the Twelve and the Seventy. When Jesus sent forth His 12 disciples, it could conceivably be understood as an isolated situation. But in sending the Seventy, He undoubtedly meant it to be a pattern of the work and the workers throughout the following centuries.

In sending out the Seventy, Christ commanded them to pray that others likewise would be sent forth. The Seventy were pioneers in a mighty army that in the ensuing years would follow in their train. Notice that the Seventy were to precede Christ. They were to go to every city that Christ intended to visit. So we in our missionary work simply go before Christ. He will follow up our work. In a little while He will return in person with His rewards. We are the forerunners of the Lord's coming.

Those Seventy were to be self-denying and simple of lifestyle. In these respects, too, they were patterns of all true missionaries. They were not to carry needless baggage or look for earthly luxuries and comforts. They were light infantry intended to itinerate rapidly and cover the land with the message of Christ's return. Oh, that all our missionaries were like them!

The Seventy were to go out two-by-two. The Lord still sends His disciples in company. And they were to go armed with the power to tread on serpents and scorpions, power to withstand their archenemy, Satan. Yet the fact that demons were subject to them was far less significant than that their names were written in heaven.

Step 4: Obey Christ's Great Commission

The next step involves the great public commission that Christ gave following His resurrection. "Go ye therefore, and teach all nations" (Matthew 28:19). It was His great manifesto as King. He was about to ascend to His throne. Before doing so He proclaimed: "All power is given unto me in heaven and in earth" (28:18). And with that proclamation He sent forth His ambassadors to call the nations of earth to His kingdom. They were to teach observance of all Jesus' commands to the very end.

Jesus accompanied His commission with the promise of His providential presence. It is a presence that carries with it all the omnipotence of the Godhead. It is an unfailing presence that none can claim in its fullness if they are not obeying the command that precedes it.

Jesus' Great Commission has never yet been fully realized. It contemplates a worldwide evangelization so glorious and complete that no nation, tribe or tongue will be overlooked! It calls us to focus especially on the nations rather than on the isolated individual; unevangelized peoples should be the first objects of our care. Nor are we to rest until this glorious gospel shall have been proclaimed in every tongue spoken by man. God wants representatives from every nation to herald the return of the Son of Man!

Step 5: Obey Jesus' personal commission

Next comes the personal commission. "Go ye into all the world," Jesus said, "and preach the gospel to every creature. He that believeth and is baptized shall be saved; but he that believeth not shall be damned" (Mark 16:15–16). It is Jesus' commission to the individual to go to the individual. Every member of the human family has a right to know the way of life. The world will never be evangelized until every individual Christian recognizes his or her personal missionary call. Jesus has already called; if we cannot go personally, we must see that someone goes to represent us.

This personal commission is the most solemn and searching word on the subject of missions in the whole Bible. It will meet each one of us on the judgment day. No person, no church can absolve us from our eternal obligation or excuse us from our duty.

Step 6: Recognize the divine priority

The divine order of the gospel message needs our attention. In Luke 14:16–24 we can read Jesus' parable of the great supper. Inherent in that story is His plan for the evangelization of the world.

The first invited guests represent the ordinary hearers of the gospel. God sends the message to them, but they are too busy with worldly interests and their pleasures to respond. So God calls again: "Go out quickly into the streets and lanes of the city, and bring in hither the poor, and the maimed, and the halt, and the blind." This time God reaches out to the neglected ones within a local area. This corresponds to the work of rescue missions and home missions. They are extremely important, but they are not all.

There is a third call: "Go out into the highways and hedges"—to the outcasts, to the people beyond the immediate influence of the church. This is the cross-cultural outreach that we are endeavoring to carry out. God requires no person to spend his or her life reiterating the gospel to people who will not receive it. He wants everyone to have an opportunity to hear. Then He would have us move on to other areas. The mistake of the church has been that she sits down to convert all the people in one country to the neglect of the great masses who have never had the chance to hear the gospel—not even once!

Step 7: Receive God's enduement of power

The enduement of power for missionary work is essential. "Ye shall receive power, after that the Holy Ghost is come upon you," Jesus promised: "and ye shall be witnesses unto me both in Jerusalem and in all Judaea, and in Samaria, and unto the uttermost part of the earth" (Acts 1:8).

The mighty undertaking that the Master was committing to His followers was beyond their power.

Therefore He provided for them the infinite resources of the Holy Spirit. The Holy Spirit was to convince the world of sin, of righteousness and of judgment. And, indeed, He did accompany the apostles in their ministry — frequently with stupendous power and astonishing results.

Peter's sermon in Jerusalem on the day of Pentecost brought conviction to thousands. In the course of a single missionary journey, the apostle Paul established Christianity throughout Asia Minor. In another tour, the great and civilized communities of Greece were led to accept the truth, and powerful churches were established in all the leading cities.

Paul declares how in Thessalonica he proclaimed the truth by the power of the Holy Spirit sent down from heaven. Multitudes turned from their idols to serve the living and true God and to wait for His Son from heaven. The apostle's speech, delivered in the power of the Holy Spirit, stirred and persuaded the hearts of men and women. At Corinth, too, Paul reminds the church that he came not with excellency of speech or human wisdom, but in demonstration of the Spirit's power (see 1 Corinthians 2:4).

This same mighty power is as necessary today in the midst of our ecclesiastical machinery. We are in danger of forgetting it. Modern schools, medical missions, industrial teaching and a thousand other things can never take the place of the filling of the Holy Spirit. Nor will the fullness of this power ever be known except in connection with world evangelization. It is for this that Christ especially promised it. As we seek this power for witnessing of Him, we may claim it without limitation. The wider our witness, the more glorious the power.

In Ezekiel's celebrated vision, the prophet watched as God transformed an army of bleached bones into enfleshed cadavers. But death still reigned. Then, suddenly, the call: "Come from the four winds, O breath, and breathe upon these slain, that they may live" (Ezekiel 37:9). And, lo! as the rushing wind swept from every side and breathed life into those passive forms, they sprang to their feet and stood in ranks, "an exceeding great army." So today, a few thousand men and women have stepped out in front of the armies of the living God to hold the outposts around the globe. Behind them lie millions and millions not more than half alive, languidly going through the forms of battle.

Oh for the trumpet of God to wake the dead! Oh for the breath of power to rouse the great host! Oh for thousands of missionaries in every land, alive with the Holy Spirit! From the workers on every field, from the converts they have won comes one cry above all others: "Pray for us that we may be filled with the Holy Spirit!" Let us pray for them with overflowing hearts. May the mighty baptism of a missionary Pentecost begin at home and sweep in waves of fire until it encircles the earth with the mighty evangel and rolls on to meet the armies of the Advent!

Step 8: Expect supernatural signs

The special and supernatural signs that the Lord has promised will follow the preaching of the gospel. Our Lord said, "In my name shall they cast out devils; they shall speak with new tongues; they shall take up serpents; and if they drink any deadly thing, it shall not hurt them; they shall lay hands on the sick, and they shall recover." (Mark 16:17–18). Mark summarizes what happened by adding, "They went forth, and preached every where, the Lord working with them, and confirming the word with signs following" (16:20).

We get what we believe for. Since the church has, in a great measure, lost its faith in the supernatural signs and workings of the Holy Spirit, it has lost the signs, also. As a result, it is compelled to produce conviction upon the minds of the lost by purely rational and moral considerations. We seldom witness the direct appeal to the supernatural power of God that the apostles constantly called on.

The need for these supernatural evidences among those unaquainted with the gospel is as great as ever. The Brahmins of India can reason as well as we. The Chinese are as intellectual as we are. The literature of some non-Christian nations can match our own in subtlety and sophistry. But when God enters the scene with signs and wonders, people are without argument. In the touch of God there is something that man cannot answer or explain away.

We are not sent abroad to preach signs, or to initiate signs or to produce signs in and of ourselves. Our work is to tell the simple story of Jesus' life and death and resurrection—to preach the gospel in its purity. But we are to do it expecting the Lord to prove the reality of His power and to give the signs that He has promised.

In order to do this there must be faith, not only on the part of the isolated missionary but also on the part of those who sent him. There must be the united expectancy of the missionary abroad and the church at home reaching across and around the world, touching heaven with a chain of believing prayer. The perils of dangerous climates and the difficulties that confront us can become occasions for yet greater victories for the name of Jesus and mightier displays of the divine omnipotence.

God is calling us to be the instruments and channels through whom He can speak to the nations. When we are prepared to understand Him and answer His call, even a very few of us will be mightier than millions. God used a Daniel in Babylon, a Nehemiah in Jerusalem, an Esther in Iran. These operated through simple and divine faith in Him to accomplish more for His glory with great nations and empires than the whole kingdom of Judah had been able to accomplish in many centuries.

There are dangers of excess and fanaticism, admittedly. By these the enemy will try to destroy that which is true and prejudice that which is genuine. But there is a middle ground of supernatural reality and power where we may safely stand. We should stay as far from unscriptural fanaticism as we do from the coldness of unbelief. We cannot expect the power of God to be manifested at the caprice of men as a mere novelty. But where the conditions are properly met in simple, holy, humble faith, God will not disappoint His trusting children. As always in the past, He will prove that "Jesus Christ [is] the same yesterday, and to day, and for ever" (Hebrews 13:8).

Step 9: Prepare the home base

There needs to be preparation here in the homeland. God did not begin foreign missions immediately upon the founding of the apostolic church. The church was not ready. Nor was conservative Jerusalem the place. God created first a new center in Antioch, a mixed community of Gentiles and Jews comprising all social classes. There were some in the church who belonged to Herod's court. There was the scholarly Saul of Tarsus and the businessman Barnabas. Simeon was a black. There was a freedom, a simplicity, a largeness and freshness about the church in Antioch that brought it in touch with the great outlying world. And it was from that center that God began the great missionary movement from which our own evangelization has come and which today is broadening into the evangelization of the whole world.

All of this has its parallel in the church today. It is not possible through a cold, conservative ecclesiasticism to develop a true missionary movement. The work at home will always be reproduced abroad. Therefore God has been raising up in the home field not a new sect but a new spiritual movement in all the churches. It is a church within a church—a spiritual company bound together by invisible cords touching hearts and hands in the Holy Spirit. From these consecrated circles He is launching a new missionary movement. Men and women filled with the Holy Spirit are giving their lives to the work.

People ask us how it is that money can be so easily obtained and in such large sums. Back of it lies a deep spiritual cause. It is the work of many years, a glorious movement that has been deepening the life and love of God in Christian hearts. No gift or sacrifice is for one moment comparable to the blessing they have received. It would be impossible to go to a wealthy congregation and obtain any such offerings unless the people had been previously prepared by the Holy Spirit. These who give have first given themselves and all they have to the Lord. They have found in Him a life and a joy that nothing can recompense. They are glad to give all they possess to send abroad the gospel and to share this blessedness with others. And the work abroad that grows out of such lives will be living, supernatural, aggressive and wholehearted.

Step 10: Reach out ever farther

The spirit of New Testament missions is aggressive, ever reaching out "to preach the gospel in the regions beyond" (2 Corinthians 10:16). Such was the spirit of Paul's ministry. He sought out unoccupied fields. He was not satisfied while there was still another land or tribe that had not received the gospel.

And after all these intervening centuries there are still regions beyond for us to reach out to. Of the world's 3,000 languages, many hundreds yet remain into which the Bible has not been translated. Surely every true believer must understand the aspiration of the great apostle and long to break away from the old, trodden paths where so many are competing for a place, and to reach those who have had little or no opportunity to hear of salvation. May we claim whole tribes and nations for our inheritance and our spiritual offspring—jewels that we and our precious Lord will together share through the ages of glory as recompense of our labors.

Step 11: Comprehend God's missionary plan

In Acts 15:14–17, God reveals to us His plan for Christian missions. He "did visit the Gentiles, to take out of them a people for his name." But He declares, "After this I will return, and will build again the tabernacle of David, which is fallen down; and I will build again the ruins thereof, and I will set it up: that the residue of men might seek after the Lord, and all the Gentiles, upon whom my name is called."

Here are three distinct stages. First God visits the Gentiles to take out of them a people for His name. This He is doing in the missionary work of today. After this He returns to restore Israel and to build again the tabernacle of His ancient people. This is His second coming for which we are looking and waiting. Then after His coming, the residue of men and all the Gentiles will seek and find Him. In the millennial age the knowledge of the Lord will cover the earth as the waters cover the sea.

This is the divine order. Today God is visiting the Gentiles, selecting those who are willing to respond. It is a spiritual preparation for Christ's advent. He is gathering an escort who shall be able to herald, in every spoken tongue, the coming King. These will stand in glorious ranks around His millennial throne as the firstfruits of the nations.

This is our mighty calling—to find a bride for Jesus. We are called to invite the ones and twos and threes here and there to meet Him. Let us not be surprised if the multitudes decline. They are declining here at home, and they will decline in the lands abroad, too. We will not be depressed if the world refuses to accept its Lord. It has always done so, and it will do so until He comes. Our task is to sow the seed in every field and furrow. Much of it may be plucked by the birds of the air. Some of the tender plants will be choked by thorns or wither in the rocky soil. But some will bear fruit, and the Master's expectation will not be disappointed!

Step 12: Make the consummation the objective

Finally the end comes — the consummation. "This gospel of the kingdom shall be preached in all the world for a witness unto all nations; and then shall the end come" (Matthew 24:14). We are preaching the gospel not for the conversion of the world but for a witness unto all nations. When we shall have accomplished this, our Lord will come.

In effect, God has given *us* the key to the future. His great chronometer does not measure time by days and years but by preparations for the marriage of the Lamb and the readiness of the bride. How this should stir us with holy energy and aspiration! I cannot understand how any man or woman can believe in the Lord's coming and not be a missionary — or at least be committed to the work of missions — with every power of his or her being. There is no mockery more sad and inconsistent than for a believer to speak of the blessed hope with folded hands and selfish heart.

No one can rightly believe in the coming of Jesus without expending all the strength of his or her being in preparing for it by sending the gospel to all the nations. God is summoning to a great missionary crusade those who hold this hope today.

> The Master's coming draweth near,
> The Son of Man will soon appear;
>   His kingdom is at hand.
> But ere that glorious day can be,
> This gospel of the kingdom we
>   Must preach in every land.
> Oh, let us then His coming haste,
> Oh, let us end this awful waste
>   Of souls that never die.

A thousand million still are lost,
A Savior's blood has paid the cost,
   Oh, hear their dying cry!

New Testament Missionary Models

ELEVEN NEW TESTAMENT MISSIONARIES in the history of early Christianity stand out in bold relief. Each of them represents some special feature of missionary life and service.

Philip, the missionary evangelist

In Samaria, Philip had been greatly honored by God. Under his evangelistic preaching large numbers heard about Christ Jesus and gave heed to what Philip said (Acts 8:5–6). Suddenly, at the very height of the campaign, an angel of the Lord commanded Philip, one of the original Jerusalem deacons (Acts 6:5), to leave his fruitful work and go down to the desert road that leads from Jerusalem to Gaza.

If ever a man could have been excused for staying at home and taking care of an overflowing spiritual harvest, it was Philip. But not for a moment did he hesitate. Promptly he left his work and, like Abraham, started out not knowing exactly where or why.

A cloud of dust on the distant horizon heralded a coming cavalcade. Soon Philip was facing the chariot of an important Ethiopian official. The man was returning from Jerusalem to his distant North African home, disappointed and still spiritually hungry. Vainly he had sought in Jerusalem, the great religious metropolis, a healing balm for his broken heart. He had the Book of God, but he needed a living voice to interpret it.

"Understandest thou what thou readest?" Philip asked.

"How can I," the Ethiopian replied, "except some man should guide me?" And "Philip opened his mouth, and . . . preached unto him Jesus" (8:35).

It was a simple sermon—all about Jesus—to a single hearer. The African received the word and asked then and there to be baptized. And from that encounter the Ethiopian official continued on his way rejoicing to relay the Good News to his fellow Africans.

Many are the lessons expressed in that compelling account. There is the need for a missionary call, and there is the necessity of prompt obedience when it comes. There is the demand of faith when God's leading seems to dead-end in a wilderness. There is the need to discern opportunities. There is the obvious value of the individual. And when God converts people, we need to entrust them to the Lord and let them go on their way rejoicing.

But above all other lessons in this episode from Philip's life is the supreme claim of foreign missionary work above all other calls, all other needs. For Philip it warranted his leaving a great work in Samaria to minister to a single foreign citizen seeking after God. In the light of this example, is there anything as important, as transcendent as world evangelization?

Barnabas, the consecrated businessman

The Scriptures afford us sufficient glimpses of

Barnabas to justify our conclusion that he probably was a successful businessman. Certainly he was a man of wealth and property. Our very introduction to him discloses the information that "having land, [he] sold it, and brought the money, and laid it at the apostles' feet" (Acts 4:37). The firstfruit of his consecration was the giving of his wealth to the cause of Christ. God gloriously honored him not only by taking his gifts but by receiving the man himself. Not too much later he and Paul became the first missionaries sent out by the church to inaugurate the great work of world evangelization. Philip had gone as an individual and temporarily. But Barnabas and Paul began the first organized missionary work of the church. Barnabas, therefore, stands for all that is most practical and devoted in the Christian layman.

Through the ages God has used such men and women. It takes more than ministers to constitute the missionary army. Philip of Saxony was as necessary to the Reformation as Martin Luther. Robert and Alexander Haldane were as essential to Scotland's revival as Knox and Peden. Lord Shaftsbury, William Wilberforce and Count von Zinzendorf were as much the anointed of the Lord as were Wesley, Baxter and Spurgeon.

Today many of the most useful and honored missionaries are men and women who have gone abroad from secular callings. They have taken into the Master's work the strength, the sterling qualities, the practical wisdom which business life has taught them. Someone has aptly remarked that the significant part of modern commerce is not the vast fortunes some have accumulated but rather the splendid genius that has made such fortunes and invested them. God wanted Barnabas much more than He wanted his money. He wanted Barnabas's ability, his energy, his wisdom, influence and experience. He wanted these for the counsels of His kingdom. The chief value of our financial gift to God lies in its proof that we ourselves belong to God unreservedly.

Industrialist, businessperson, professional, are you doing your best for your Redeemer and the cause of world evangelization? The Lord has need of you!

Gaius, missionary host

There is no more attractive figure in the New Testament than the noble Christian gentleman whom the apostle John introduces to us in his third letter. In strong, striking words he tells us what kind of a man he was: "The brethren came and testified of the truth that is in thee, even as thou walkest in the truth. I have no greater joy than to hear that my children walk in truth. Beloved, thou doest faithfully whatsoever thou doest to the brethren, and to strangers; which have borne witness of thy charity before the church" (3 John 3–6).

But John also lets us glimpse the relation this good man had to the missionaries of Christ. First he remarks how they went forth in a spirit of self-sacrifice and faith in God. They asked nothing from the spiritually lost to whom they carried the message of the gospel. "For [Jesus'] name's sake they went forth, taking nothing of the Gentiles" (verse 7). And John reminds Gaius of the duty he and fellow believers have to such missionaries. "Whom if thou bring forward on their journey after a godly sort, thou shalt do well. . . . We therefore ought to receive such, that we might be fellowhelpers to the truth" (verses 6, 8).

It is a fitting picture of the duty Christians and churches in the homeland have to the foreign missionary. The missionary is to go forth in self-sacrificing love and simple faith, "taking nothing of the Gentiles." Those at home are to be fellow helpers, receiving such and "bring[ing] them forward on their journey after a godly sort."

This is what we are doing when we help an earnest, consecrated student through his course of training, help supply his outfit, transportation and monthly support. This is the principle David enunciated to his men: "As his part is that goeth down to the battle, so shall his part be that tarrieth by the stuff: they shall part alike" (1 Samuel 30:24). God has not given you money so that you might hoard it for your own interests, putting it in a savings bank or in stocks and bonds. God has committed to the great body of His people here at home a partnership and a trust. Are we fulfilling it like Gaius, the missionaries' host, fellow-helper and supporting friend?

Epaphras, missionary prayer partner

No missionary force is more prevailing than prayer. The art of powerful praying has been learned by only a few. Those few are God's special priests and priestesses, who stand with holy hands at the footstool of God's throne, sharing the intercession of Jesus, the great High Priest. Some day we shall discover that these are the greatest missionaries of all.

Epaphras was such a person. Paul used forceful language when he described his praying. There are several Greek words for prayer, but the one used about Epaphras's prayers is the strongest of all. It expresses the kind of entreaty that presses its case until the most difficult situation has been prayed through. "Laboring fervently for you in prayers," Paul put it (Colossians 4:12).

Have you found your place at the throne of intercession? It was the Master's special commission to His disciples: "Pray ye the Lord of the harvest, that he will send forth labourers into his harvest" (Matthew 9:38). It is the ministry that will bring workers of the right kind and money from consecrated hearts and hands. It will open the doors of every land and the hearts of every race. Prayer will bring down the latter rain in floods upon the dry ground. None may be barred from this ministry. You may be too old to go overseas as a missionary. You may be too poor to give very much. But if you will dedicate your heart to Christ for the priesthood of prayer, you may bring blessings upon the world that will make your single life worth a thousand lives.

Charles Finney tells of a retired man in Ohio who, laid aside by infirmity, nevertheless received a filling of the Holy Spirit that took the special form of prayer for the lost world and the work of God. It was the man's custom to take up individual congregations, ministers and mission fields in turn and pray for God to send revival to each. He kept a diary of these seasons of prayer. When after his death the diary was examined, it was discovered that a wave of revival had traveled around the world in the exact order of the man's prayers.

Oh, Epaphras, the Lord has need of *you*. You may be a modest young woman, an aging mother, a worn-out preacher, a humble disciple. But to you it may be given to turn the key that will unlock world revival and bring back our returning Lord!

Luke, the literature missionary

For awakening missionary interest and summoning workers to the harvest fields of earth there is still no more effective medium than the printed page and the consecrated pen. Luke pioneered the missionary press. It was he who gave us The Acts. He wrote 28 glowing chapters and then left the book unfinished for us to complete the story. Ours will not be the acts of the apostles but the acts of the Holy Spirit and the ascended Christ.

Do not be like the one-talent man and protest your inability to write. The missionary press is looking not so much for writers as for readers. It is the missionary-minded *reader* who supports missionary literature. Back the cause of missions by subscribing to several missionary periodicals. Do it if for no other reason than to encourage and sustain these worthy organizations in their fruitful ministry of calling candidates and gathering money for the work of world evangelization. Better still, you can circulate these periodicals, passing them on to others to whom they may prove as great a blessing as they were to you.

A few months ago a fragment of one of our Christian and Missionary Alliance papers, blown along the roadside, was picked up by a Christian who was hungering for the kind of truth the page contained. As a result, he subscribed to the magazine. And in course of time he donated, out of a grateful heart, several thousands of dollars to our work.

Not many months earlier, a quiet Christian woman in the far South, who had not heard of our work before, picked up a leaflet describing The Christian and Missionary Alliance. Within a few days she had contributed enough money to support two missionaries for a whole year!

Are you helping the ministry of the missionary press?

Aquila and Priscilla, missionaries in the home

Aquila and Priscilla are in a class of their own. They were not sent by any missionary organization. They were not dependent upon the support of a church or churches. They were just a plain business couple who took care of themselves. As God moved them from city to city, they simply let their light shine for Him. The result was an important impact on others, including a gifted evangelist. Apollos, perhaps second only to Paul in ability, was led into the fullness of Jesus through Priscilla and Aquila.

Speaking of Aquila and Priscilla, Paul declared that they had "laid down their own necks" for him (Romans 16:4). Not only did he give thanks to God for them, but so did "all the churches of the Gentiles." Aquila and Priscilla represent what we might call the self-supporting, "tent-making" missionary (they were tent-makers, like Paul). They reflected the beauty and glory of Christ in the godless world around them.

When Commodore Matthew Calbraith Perry, who opened Japan to American commerce, was asked what he thought of missionaries, he answered, "I myself am a missionary." We do not need holy orders to set us apart for God. The orders of the Holy Spirit are enough. It would be a glorious ministry for the gospel and the world if a large number of men and women with sufficient financial support and no pressing need to remain at home, would simply move to

the overseas world and live there at their own expense
as witnesses for Christ.

Timothy, the missionary helper

Timothy was a young man of exceptional back-
ground and gifts. But he was quite willing to be second in rank — a humble helper to Paul the apostle.

There are too many captains around. God wants
more privates willing to follow in the ranks and take
the lowly place. Only these can be leaders themselves,
for "whosoever shall exalt himself shall be abased; and
he that shall humble himself shall be exalted" (Matthew 23:12).

Epaphroditus, the missionary generalist

Paul has given us a complimentary description of
Epaphroditus in his letter to the Philippians: "I sup-
posed it necessary to send to you Epaphroditus, my
brother, and companion in labour, and fellowsoldier,
but your messenger, and he that ministered to my
wants. For he longed after you all, and was full of
heaviness, because that ye had heard that he had been
sick. . . . For the work of Christ he was nigh unto
death, not regarding his life, to supply your lack of
service toward me" (2:26–30).

Epaphroditus was one of those all-around workers
who was ready for any ministry that was most
needed. Not only was he ready to preach the gospel,
but to seek for and find a suffering prisoner in a Roman dungeon and wait on him with his own hands.
So unselfish was Epaphroditus that he became exceedingly ill through exposure and overexertion. Instead of asking for sympathy, his one concern was to

keep his friends from finding out lest they should be unduly anxious about him.

We need people like Epaphroditus on the mission field. We need all-around people who can wait by the bedside of a sick and suffering missionary, minister to a pagan child, help in the housekeeping at a missionary guest house, assist with construction projects or be a general worker wherever the need is greatest. May God give us more Epaphrodituses!

Mark, the restored missionary

John Mark was one of those ardent, enthusiastic young fellows who respond eagerly under the first impulses of their hearts. But when Mark was confronted with the difficulties of missionary work, he was just as eager to get back home to his mother. There are John Marks in every generation.

We are prone to be discouraged and sometimes upset with these missionary failures. Like Paul with Mark, we feel like rejecting them as worthless material. But the story of Mark is instructive. It reminds us that we must have the patience of Barnabas, be willing to give these so-called "failures" a second chance. Paul was later to say of Mark, "He is profitable to me for the ministry" (2 Timothy 4:11).

Some of us never learn anything well until we have failed and started again at the bottom. It takes a good tumble to bring us to the bottom, and the second chance sometimes brings out the best. Thank God, there *is* a second chance for the contrite person!

Persis, the woman missionary

We must not overlook the women. The only person in Paul's catalog of friends at Rome to get a double mark of commendation is "the beloved Persis, which laboured much in the Lord" (Romans 16:12). Others labored, but she labored much. It is usually a woman who reaches the superlative degree.

Beginning with Mary Magdalene, the first missionary of the cross, what a glorious chain of loving, consecrated women leads on through the ages! We might pick out Mary of Jerusalem, the mother of Mark and sister of Barnabas, who seems to have been hostess to the apostolic church. Surely we could not pass by Priscilla, the spiritual mother of Apollos and the trusted friend of Paul. In this same glorious company we find Lydia of Philippi, little Rhoda, Phebe of Cenchrea, Mary of Rome and many others.

Thank God, the species is not extinct. The missionary work of women is wider, deeper and more glorious today than ever before. No one can do more in promoting missions at home. No one can be such an effective recruiting agent for missionaries, especially in her own family. No one can give more sacrificially. God help you, beloved Persises, as you labor much in the Lord.

Paul, the pioneer missionary

How shall we in a few sentences picture the prince of missionaries, who in himself summed up all the qualities, characteristics and types of spiritual power for missionary service? We cannot. So let us concentrate on one feature of Paul's ministry in which he excelled above others: he pioneered. He was the great pathfinder in an unexplored world of non-Christian men and women. It was his calling to blaze a trail through the dark recesses of earth's benighted regions.

Paul's one intense desire and instinctive impulse was to preach the gospel where Christ had not been named (Romans 15:20). The desire that drove him was that of reaching out to the regions beyond him. He had no time to linger with cherished friends or in congenial surroundings as long as there was a human being within his reach to whom the story of Jesus had not been told.

It is almost with amusement that we hear Paul say to the Romans, "Now having no more place in these parts, . . . whensoever I take my journey into Spain, I will come to you" (Romans 15:23–24). He would not take the time to go to Rome until he had discharged his responsibility to the area right around him—until he had "fully preached the gospel of Christ" in the whole region "from Jerusalem, and round about until Illyricum" (Romans 15:19).

What a perfect model for young people today as God opens up new areas for the soldiers of the cross to conquer. In fact, what fitting models are all 11 of these New Testament missionaries. The voice of a sublime ambition is summoning us to march under Christ's banner. Let us enter the world's open doors for the last campaign of this Christian age and the final triumph of the Lamb.

The Logic of Missions

Paul's chain of inexorable logic, preserved for us in Romans 10:14–15, sums up the whole practical side of missions. It brings home the guilt of the world's moral, spiritual and eternal ruin to the conscience of every man and woman who is not doing his or her best to send the gospel of Jesus Christ to all mankind. Here is how he puts it:

> *How then shall they call on him in whom they have not believed? and how shall they believe in him of whom they have not heard? and how shall they hear without a preacher? And how shall they preach, except they be sent? as it is written, How beautiful are the feet of them that preach the gospel of peace, and bring glad tidings of good things! (Romans 10:14–15)*

There is no sentiment about this. It is stern, unyielding logic, and it brings every one of us, by an irresistible argument, face to face with the responsibility of the world's ruin or redemption. It tells us that God has provided a remedy sufficient and completely fitted for all the wants of our fallen race. He has given us a salvation that is adequate, adapted and designed for all the world. He has put the simple conditions of it within the reach of every person who hears the gospel. Now, to use an expressive colloquial phrase, "it is up to you"—and me—whether people shall be lost or saved. Let us look at this magnificent argument.

Paul always begins with the heart. He starts with a great burst of love for his lost brethren. "Brethren, my heart's desire and prayer to God for Israel is, that they might be saved" (Romans 10:1). This is the motivating power of missionary work—a heart aflame with love for people and a longing to lead them to Christ.

The gospel for the world

But mere sentiment cannot save a lost world. The tenderest love and most self-denying sacrifices cannot lift our lost humanity from the fearful effects of the Fall. It needs a divine remedy, a gospel of superhuman power as well as divine compassion.

The Apostle Paul had discovered such a gospel and had been commissioned to declare to men such a remedy. This remedy and gospel were so incomparably superior to all that the world had found, up to that point in time, that he was enthusiastic in his desire to proclaim it to all men.

He had found a panacea for all human sin and sorrow, and it was so good that he could not bear to have a single human being miss it. He expressed it by one great word which was a favorite of his and which we find again and again in his epistle to the Romans. It is the word "righteousness." Earlier in his letter, in a well-known passage, he put it this way: "But now the righteousness of God without the law is manifested" (Romans 3:21). Later he expressed the idea again: "Christ is the end of the law for righteousness to

every one that believeth" (10:4). That term, "righteousness," simply means rightness. The idea is that
God has provided a plan for righting every wrong of
humanity.

It was said of the apostles, "These that have turned
the world upside down are come hither" (Acts 17:6).
There is a story told of an eccentric English evangelist
who took that text for one of his open-air sermons in
a new place. He began by saying, "First, the world is
wrong side up. Second, the world must be turned
upside down. Third, we are the men to set it right."
Such is really the purpose of the gospel. It is God's
way of making things right.

Things are wrong between the world and God. The
world does not know Him. Its citizens do not love
Him. They do not trust Him. They cannot stand before Him with acceptance. Their sins have separated
them from God, and the guilt of sin is bearing them
down to deeper sin and a dark eternal hell. But God
has sent Jesus Christ to make this right. He has become a Man and as such represents the fallen human
family. As the great representative Man, He has taken
upon Himself man's sins, man's obligations, man's
wrongs against God. He has met the issue, and He has
paid the penalty. He has lived up to the requirements
of God's most perfect law and has thus wrought out a
righteousness that is perfect and sufficient to cover all
the guilt of fallen man and forever to settle the salvation of every sinner who will accept this settlement.
This is the gospel of salvation through the blood and
righteousness of Jesus Christ. It is the only remedy
for a guilty conscience and a sinful heart. It is the
power of God unto salvation to everyone that be-
lieves, and it was Paul's delight to go to the known

world and tell sinful men of the glorious righteousness of God.

But God's righteousness is more than this. It is also
His provision for taking away the sin of the human
heart and giving to weak, fallen man the power to be
right toward Him and toward all men. The worst
thing in our fallen state is not our guilt and our liabil-
ity to eternal punishment. The worst thing is our
helplessness to do right or even want to do right.

We are told that those who do not know of the true
God will be saved if they will live up to the light they
have. We do not stop to question this, for God will
surely do right by every righteous man. But the diffi-
culty is that no one can do right of himself or herself.
We — with the gospel light — cannot do right. Human
nature is helpless, and the very essence of the gospel is
that it gives the power to choose and do the right.
God takes away the love of sin; He makes us love the
things that He loves and hate the things He hates. He
has power to cleanse, purify and uplift human nature.
He is a divine force placed within the human heart,
that causes us to walk in His statutes and keep His
commandments. This is the gospel we are called to
give to a lost world: the righteousness of God. This is
the glory of the gospel, and with such a remedy for
the dark stains of humanity, what a cruel crime it is to
keep it back from our struggling and sinking fellow
man.

All this comes through Christ

This righteousness is not character slowly built up.
It is not mere merit painfully attained as the Buddhist
tries to attain it. It is a Person, a living, loving, real
Man, Christ, our Brother, our Savior, our living

Head, who has fashioned it all out for us and who waits to give it to us the moment we accept Him. It is not a struggle to be good in our own strength, but a simple act of confidence in a loving Redeemer who undertakes the whole task for us and gives to us a free gift of righteousness the moment we accept Him.

Christ is the world's answer, the world's remedy, the world's hope, the world's Redeemer. The apostle's one business was to minister Christ to men and women, to tell them of Jesus and bring them into contact with Him who is the desire of the nations and the remedy for all man's wrongs. All this is without the law and by the free grace of God. "Christ is the end of the law for righteousness to every one that believeth" (Romans 10:4).

When we receive Him, we pass from under the condemnation, the claims, the terrors of the law. We do not have to obey a stern commandment as a condition of salvation, but we receive a righteousness, higher than man himself could ever have attained, as the free gift of His grace. His merits become ours, and we stand before God in as good a place as if we had never sinned, in as good a place as if we had done everything that He has done and kept every commandment that He has kept. Not only so, we receive Him into our hearts as a living Presence, an efficient Power, a divine Enabling, and united to Him we can relive the life He lived and be even as He was in this world.

Such a salvation, so complete, so sufficient, so far-reaching, so free, is enough to set on fire the hearts of angels and to make us human beings who have received it burn with desire to pass it on to all the race.

What a pity that this lost world should be another hour without it.

An accessible righteousness

This righteousness is accessible and available to all people. It is not far off, but near. It is not hung high in the heavens where sinners must painfully climb the heights of virtue and achievement before they can attain it, but it reaches down to the level of the most lost and helpless of men. Its terms are as simple as language can express or love can provide. It says, "Whosoever shall call on the name of the Lord shall be saved" (Acts 2:21). There is nothing so easy as to call, to utter a cry of need and know that instantly the love and grace of God will respond. It is not restricted to any class or race: "There is no difference . . . for the same Lord over all is rich unto all that call upon him" (Romans 10:12). It is not for moral Jew or cultivated Greek or initiated philosopher, but it is for the common people, the sinful people, the "whosoever will."

He uses a beautiful figure to express its accessibility:

> *Say not in thine heart, Who shall ascend into heaven? (that is, to bring Christ down from above:) Or, Who shall descend into the deep? (that is, to bring up Christ again from the dead.) But what saith it? The word is nigh thee, even in thy mouth, and in thy heart: that is, the word of faith, which we preach; that if thou shalt confess with thy mouth the Lord Jesus, and shalt believe in thine heart that God hath raised him from the dead, thou shalt be saved (Romans 10:6–9).*

A person does not need to slowly climb to some high experience to be able to know God and become righteous, as the ancient philosophers taught. He does not need to go down to some depth of abasement to make himself worthy of God's mercy. All the efforts which the false religions and cults inflict upon their votaries as a meritorious cause of salvation are foolish and needless. Just where the repentant sinner is this moment, he can meet Jesus and sing: "This uttermost salvation, / It reaches me."

Altar of earth

Even amid all the wreck of humanity, there is still in every human heart some echo of the voice of God, some sense of need, some responsive touch that the gospel awakens, meets and satisfies. There is a description in Exodus of the nearness of God to sinful people. It comes at the close of chapter 20, immediately after the sublime and awful picture of Mt. Sinai and the terrors of the ancient law. Just at the foot of that fiery mount of judgment, God provided the Israelites with an example of His grace, full of the very spirit of the gospel. It was an altar of earth representing the place where sinful men were to meet the God of this fiery law. They could not meet Him on the fearful top of Sinai, for that only spoke of judgment. But this altar of earth represented the cross of Calvary and the plan of salvation through the blood of Jesus Christ. There they were to bring their bleeding sacrifices and find atonement for the sin which the law so fearfully condemned.

The description of the altar is a very poem of grace. First, it was to be built not of stone but of earth, the commonest, least expensive material within the reach of everybody. Second, if it was to be made of stone, it must be of stones as they were found, for God said, "If thou lift up thy tool upon it, thou hast polluted it"

(v. 25). No works of man must mingle with the free grace which insists upon saving us alone.

Also, there were to be no steps leading up to the altar. There is not a single step needed to raise the sinner to a level where God can meet him. God meets each one on his own level, stooping to the lowest place where guilty sinners exist, crying, "Ho, every one that thirsteth, come ye to the waters, and he that hath no money; come ye, buy and eat; . . . without money and without price" (Isaiah 55:1).

There is another beautiful picture of the nearness of God's mercy and grace to helpless sinners in Leviticus 14. It is the picture of the poor leper outside the camp, excluded from the fellowship of his brethren by his uncleanness and leprosy. But in infinite tenderness and mercy, God is represented as going out to meet the sinner there: "the priest shall go forth to him out of the camp" (v. 3). God's mercy meets him where he lies in his separation and misery and supplies all that is necessary for his return and his future way.

God's far-reaching mercy and grace

Perhaps there has never been a finer illustration of the far-reaching mercy and grace of God to sinful men than that spoken by a certain Chinese. When asked why he had given up Confucius and Buddha and accepted Jesus Christ instead, he said: "I was down in a deep pit into which I had fallen in my folly and sin. I was sinking in the mire and vainly calling for aid. Suddenly a shadow fell across the pit. Looking up, I saw Confucius. I implored him to reach out his hand and help me, but he proceeded calmly to instruct me in the principles of right living, and told me that if I had only listened to his teaching I would not have been there. It was vain for me to cry, 'Help me, help me now! Your good advice will be useful after I get out, but it is useless until someone delivers me from this pit of death,' for he was gone, and I knew that Confucius could not save me.

"Later, another shadow fell upon the opening, and I looked up to see Buddha. With the frenzy of despair, I cried to him to save me. But Buddha folded his arms and looked serenely down upon me. 'My son,' he said, 'be quiet, be patient, be still. Don't mind your troubles, ignore them; the secret of happiness is to die to self and surroundings, to retire to the inward calm and center of your heart. There you shall find Nirvana, eternal rest, and that is the end of all existence.' As he turned to leave, I cried, 'Father, if you will only get me out of this pit, I can do all you tell me. But how can I be quiet and satisfied sinking in this awful mire?' He benignly waved his hands and said, 'My son be still, be still,' and passed on. And I knew that Buddha would not save me.

"At that point I was ready to give up hope, when a third shadow fell across my vision. I looked up and saw a Man, like myself, with kind and tender countenance. Marks of dried blood were upon his brow. He spoke to me and said, 'My child, I have come to save you. Will you let me?' I cried out in my despair, 'Come, Lord, help me, I perish!' In a moment He had leaped down into the pit and put His arms around me. He lifted me up, placed me on the brink and took from me my torn and spattered garments. He washed me and robed me in new raiment, and then He said, 'I have come to save you from your distress, and now if you will follow Me, I will never leave you. I will be your Guide and Friend all the way and will keep you from ever falling again.' His name was Jesus. I fell at His feet, saying, 'Lord, I will follow You!'

"That," said the man, "is why I became a Christian."

This same Jesus who has brought you and me out of a horrible pit and the miry clay and set our feet upon solid rock and established our goings, is longing to do the same for every lost and helpless child of our fallen race. How sad, how needless, how terrible that we should allow them to perish without ever knowing Him. How can we be so cruel to them and so heartless to Him? By the love that ransomed us, let us go, like Him, "to seek and to save that which was lost." Such is the glorious gospel which God has provided for this lost world.

Our responsibility is the whole world

There are three links in this chain of responsibility:

1. "How shall they call on him in whom they have not believed?" Believing is the responsibility of every sinner. God calls upon every lost man to believe on the Lord Jesus Christ, to call upon Him as Savior and Lord. If people refuse to do this, the responsibility for the loss of their souls is their own. They have had their chance and they have made their choice. God cannot save people without their believing in Him.

In the very nature of things there must be confidence, there must be consent, there must be response of the human will and the human heart to the call of God. Salvation is not a mechanical process, but a voluntary one. Every human effort must cooperate with God. "He that believeth on him is not condemned: but he that believeth not is condemned already, because he hath not believed in the name of the only begotten Son of God" (John 3:18). Men deserve to be lost forever if they refuse to accept the Savior who is offered to them. This is the one deciding question for every human being. No person will perish eternally on account of his sins but only on account of his treatment of Jesus Christ. It is not the sin question but the Son question. Because of that, God wants the message of salvation offered to all mankind. Then the responsibility rests with them. "Go ye into all the world, and preach the gospel to every creature. He that believeth and is baptized shall be saved; but he that believeth not shall be damned" (Mark 16:15–16).

2. The second link of responsibility is the human agency. "How shall they believe in him of whom they have not heard? And how shall they hear without a preacher?" The agency is the messenger. God has ordained the human agency as the conveyor of the gospel to mankind. He might have proclaimed it with trumpet voice, as He doubtless did when He went down into Hades and preached to the spirits in prison. He might have written it in flaring characters upon the sky. He might have sent a thousand angels to declare it among the nations. But He has chosen to give us the privilege and honor of sharing with Him in this glorious work. "Now then we are ambassadors for Christ, as though God did beseech you by us: we pray you in Christ's stead, be ye reconciled to God" (2 Corinthians 5:20). Therefore, Christ's first word to His disciples is "go." The call of the heavenly voices is, "Whom shall I send, and who will go for us?" (Isaiah 6:8). He is waiting for volunteers, and He will only send volunteers. It is the duty of everyone to go who has not a good reason for staying at home. Have we heard this call? Have we weighed our responsibility?

Have we waited for our marching orders? Are we where God wants us in this matter? Are *you*?

3. The last link brings the responsibility home to every one of us. "How shall they preach except they be sent?" Sending is something that we all can do. Certainly, it is God's business to send a messenger, and the words *apostle* and *missionary* just mean "sent ones." The 12 apostles were 12 missionaries, and every missionary should be sent by the Holy Spirit.

But it is our duty to send them too. We read in Acts that before God began the great work of modern missions, He commanded the church at Antioch to separate its two best leaders and send them forth as foreign missionaries—and it is distinctly added, "So they, being sent forth by the Holy Spirit, departed unto . . . Cyprus" (13:4). Who is to do the sending? First, the church, through its officers and missionary boards is called upon to send. And, the missionary call should always have two sides—the volunteer's side, as he offers his services, and the church's side, as it accepts him and stands with him in joint responsibility for his work and for his support.

But the parent can also send his or her child. What are you doing as parents? How are you shaping the future of your children? Are you saying, as one of our missionaries once reported an American Christian as saying to him, "Yes we believe our children should go as missionaries when God calls them, but we do not initiate the question." Is that loyalty to God? Or are you going further? Are you like the eagle that stole the lamb of sacrifice from the altar and found, when she reached her nest, that she had carried a coal from the fire along with the lamb, which in a moment burned up her nest and her young? Have you found that in robbing God of some precious life, you have wrecked that life and desolated your own home circle?

We can also support, financially, those we send. The question of money is today the deciding factor in connection with any large advance movement in the missionary field. As we sacrificially give to support the endeavor abroad, God will count our work a partnership with them, and we shall share alike in the recompense when the great harvest shall be gathered.

Are we doing our part?

Are we doing our part? Shall we do it again today to send the missionaries who bring the missing link, the touch of a human hand, the sound of a human voice, the Word of God and the voice of love to wake up the faith of the world's lost children?

A man once called on a Christian businessman, and finding him intensely busy, asked how many hours he worked daily.

"Twenty-four," the businessman responded.

"How is that possible?" asked the visitor.

"When I was a young man," the other began, "I gave my life to God for foreign missions. Soon after this, my father died, and it became necessary for me to remain at home and carry on the business as a support to my mother and sister. But I found another way of carrying out my missionary consecration.

"We have branches of our business in various parts of this country. This suggested the idea of having a missionary department with branches around the world. For example, we have a branch in southern China, another in India and still another in Africa. So while I am working here, my representatives overseas are sleeping. When I retire at night they begin work on the other side of the world, carrying with them a witness for Christ. In that way our business stays open 24 hours every day. I find these missionary branches not only give a broader scope to our business but a delightful interest and the very best returns."

That is missionary consecration put into practice. That is the meaning of a missionary pledge. We do not give on the impulse of the moment, then forget about it for 12 months. No, we must enter into a contract that runs the entire year. We carry on our business and perform our daily tasks in partnership with the Lord Jesus Christ, gaining, saving and sacrificing the fruits of our toil for the spread of the gospel and the building up of His glorious kingdom.

Christianity's Crime

ONE OF THE BIBLE'S PROVERBS COMMENTS pointedly on what I have called Christianity's crime. Here is what it says: "If thou forbear to deliver them that are drawn unto death, and those that are ready to be slain; if thou sayest, Behold, we knew it not; doth not he that pondereth the heart consider it? and he that keepeth thy soul, doth not he know it? and shall not he render to every man according to his works?" (Proverbs 24:11–12).

In that text of Scripture I see a great peril, a great neglect, an insufficient excuse, a solemn accountability. Look at them with me in that order, ponder what God has to say to you and then ask, "What am I going to do about this matter?"

A great peril

The proverb speaks of "Them that are drawn unto death, and those that are ready to be slain." The expressions might describe any great danger. Some of us have seen a man overboard at sea. How quickly the signal goes out, "Man overboard! Man overboard!" As quickly as possible the mighty engines are reversed. Life boats are lowered. Every being on board the vessel is intently absorbed in trying to save the person in the sea.

Or, of even greater concern is the pending catastrophe as a ship flounders in rough seas, the lives of its passengers and crew imperiled. Nearby ships change course as the distress signal goes out. Skilled sailors push rescue boats through the wild surf to rescue as many as possible. Friends and relatives besiege the offices of the shipping company, anxious for any shred of news. Who is there who would not do his or her best to save those lives in jeopardy?

Sometimes tragedies on a wider scale startle the world. In a moment a town is leveled by a tornado, a city by an earthquake. A flash flood inundates a wide valley, sweeping away thousands of people in a fleeting moment. How our hearts are stirred with sympathy on those occasions! We are generous in our contributions to the suffering. We move quickly to lend such assistance as we are able. What person could be so base and hardened as to refuse to help in such an hour of need?

But there is another side to human life, not less real because it is less visible. Every 15 minutes, 2,000 people* are lost forever — dead without hope of everlasting life. Every morning, the newspapers could report that enough people to populate Fresno, California or Richmond, Virginia, have perished without a ray of hope. Every New Year's Day, it could be announced without exaggeration that a population a third that of the United States has passed to an eternity of darkness and despair.

*Statistics have been updated to reflect present-day demographics.

A never-ending procession

Perhaps you have witnessed an accident or an act of violence that has left someone dead. Sickeningly you reflect that moments before, the person was full of life, able to touch and feel and think and dream. But if your eyes had been opened to see as God sees, you would have beheld not one human being but a never-ending procession of people passing to something worse than simply physical death. Their every step marked by sin and sorrow, they drop by the second into a hopeless, Christless grave.

How many, do you suppose, have passed into an eternity without God in the 63 generations of the Christian era? Dare we guess conservatively 40 billion? They wait somewhere in the realms of sorrow to meet us at the judgment seat and ask, "Why did you never tell us of salvation?"

Do you see them being "drawn to death"? Do you see them "ready to be slain"? Does there not come to your ears this sad and awful refrain:

> Oh, I seem to hear them crying
>   As they sink into the grave:
> "We are dying, we are dying!
>   Is there none to help and save?"

Think for a moment of their dreadful sorrows as they pass to that hopeless grave. As we sit in the comfort and joy of our Christian privileges and hopes, yonder in India some little girl, the brightest in her village, is being publicly dedicated to a life of prostitution as a priestess in the temple of her unholy and hideous god. At this very moment some poor child widow in one of the Oriental countries is cursing the dreadful fate that ever made her a woman. Some opium victim is dragging his emaciated form into a lonely cave to die alone.

All of this would be bearable if there was a brighter hope beyond the grave. I have seen a dying mother, her life one long, sad story of cruel victimization, passing through the gates of death with shouts of victory. All her early anguish was swallowed up by one drop of heaven's hope and joy. But these I refer to have no such hope. When they lie down to die, there is nothing but darkness and despair. There is no sweet promise to cheer them. There is no inward illumination to light up the gloom. There is no Comforter to whisper, "Fear not, I am with thee." There is no Savior to take them by the hand. Instead, around them are the horrid rites of paganism. Within their darkened hearts is nothing but the presence of evil spirits and dreadful fears and agonies. They pass from a wretched existence here into a darker future beyond.

Why do we question God's Word?

Do you say you do not believe this? That God is too merciful to let them be lost forever? That there must be some other way of hope and salvation for them?

Mark it well. This settled unbelief of God's Word probably accounts for most of our sinful neglect of the heathen world. We are pillowing our consciences on a lie. God has solemnly told us in His Word that there is no other name under heaven given among men whereby we must be saved. Only Jesus can save. The tenderest voice that ever spoke on earth declared: "Except a man be born again, he cannot see the kingdom of God" (John 3:3). If God could have saved us by some easier means, He never would have given His Son to the horrors of Calvary!

If there is *any* other way for those who have not put their trust in Christ to be saved, we had better never send them the gospel. It only increases their condemnation if they reject it. Better they should live and die in ignorance and go to heaven through God's mercy without Christ. But there is no such way! The true foundation of Divine government respecting them is given by the prophet in these unmistakable words: "If thou dost not speak to warn the wicked from his way, that wicked man shall die in his iniquity; but his blood will I require at thine hand" (Ezekiel 33:8). The meaning is unequivocal. The sinner is lost although he was unwarned. But the faithless watchman is held guilty of his blood. Those who have never trusted in Christ perish. But the church of God will be held accountable for their doom.

The picture needs one more touch if it is to be wholly accurate. We must consider the helplessness of those abroad who are perishing.

There is no one in this land of churches and Bibles who may not be saved if he or she will. But more than half the human race has had no such opportunity. Nor does it today. These have never heard of Jesus. Surely we owe them at least one chance to be saved. Talk not of the needs at home compared to most of the world abroad. The darkest scenes in New York or Chicago are as nothing when set beside vast populations in the Orient and Asia. In China alone nearly a thousand million drift into eternity, to cry as they meet their Judge, "No man cared for my soul."

Such is the awful peril of a dying world.

A great neglect

We have next in the proverb earlier quoted the picture of our inexcusable neglect of a perishing world and our indifference to its need. "If thou forbear to deliver them that are drawn to death, and those that are ready to be slain. . . . " It is not necessary to do anything to be guilty of peoples' blood. It is quite enough to do nothing—to simply let them alone. The switchman does not need to place a heavy timber across the railroad tracks to hurl a hundred lives into eternity. He only needs to neglect to close the side-track and the switch at the station. The lighthouse keeper does not need to erect false beacons to lure the unsuspecting vessel upon the reefs and rocks. He only needs to neglect to light the lamp in the lighthouse.

Some years ago a man under sentence of death was found at the last moment to be innocent. A messenger was dispatched with a pardon from the governor and told to take it where the execution was to take place. Thinking there was time enough, the messenger lingered enroute, stopping to rest and refresh himself at the wayside inn. Thoughtlessly he fell asleep. Waking suddenly, he realized his terrible error. Wildly he dashed across the countryside, renewing horses at every post. At last he dashed up to the courthouse square, loudly calling out the message of pardon he had brought. Alas! he was too late. A minute before, that innocent man had been put to death. Could the messenger ever forgive himself that crime?

I recall seeing a man who, all his life long, walked with a shadow upon his face and his head bowed under a weight of guilt. By a moment's neglect, he had once taken a human life. Oh, how men and women will go through eternity crushed with the consciousness that their selfish neglect has destined fellow beings to eternal ruin.

What if we fail to warn?

When the Johnstown, Pennsylvania, floodwaters were just beginning to pour down through the valley of death, a man on horseback was seen dashing along the course of the stream shouting at the top of his voice, "Escape for your lives! The floods! The floods! To the Hills! To the hills!" At last he, too, was overtaken by the tidal wave of destruction. But he preferred to give up his life than to let his fellow citizens perish unwarned. If we fail to offer warning, we will some day awake to see the awful meaning of what we have *not* done that we might have done.

It was not necessary that David should slay Uriah, the Hittite, with his own hand. It was sufficient that David should order him to be put in the front of the battle to perish without support. By that act David was branded as his murderer and his kingdom was blighted by the crime. It was not necessary that Ahab should stab Naboth to the heart and confiscate his vineyard. It was enough that he should let his wicked wife do it all while he lay comfortably on his couch drinking wine and listening to soft music. But Naboth's blood stained his wicked soul all the same and sent him to a dishonorable grave under the curse of an indignant heaven.

Suppose a wealthy philanthropist should leave his entire estate in the hands of a trustee to be used for the children of impoverished inner city people. And suppose that instead of using the money to help the children, the trustee spent most of the fortune on himself, buying a luxurious house and amassing all the other trappings of affluence while the children he was charged to help received little or nothing. What would society call such conduct? People would brand such a person as despicable and his actions criminal. But does that trustee's action differ from the church's and its attitude toward a world of lost men and women? God has given the gospel to the church as a trust. The church has kept it as a private luxury and let the world perish without it.

How much of the resources God has given the church has it squandered on its own aggrandizement? on selfish and needless pleasures? on work that did not need its help? Meanwhile, whole generations of people who did not have the gospel have been "drawn unto death," and God will charge the church with their blood.

Ignorance is not an excuse

The proverb earlier quoted makes it clear that ignorance is no plea. "If thou sayest, Behold, we knew it not, doth not he that pondereth the heart . . . render to every man according to his works?" The ignorance of most Christians respecting the world's need is appalling. But Christians *should* know. Suppose a family in some little town had died of starvation. All around them people living in affluence had not taken the trouble to find out the reason for the piteous cries of the starving children. Would not that community be branded by the press and public opinion as inhuman and without excuse?

We ought to know the condition of our world. God will hold us guilty for what we might have known. He has made us trustees for those who have not the gospel. It is our business to find out the needs of the world and to see that they are supplied. We are our brothers' keepers. In the great day of reckoning we shall find that our accountability will be coequal with our opportunity.

There are thousands of gospel ministers in North America who know almost nothing of the spiritual need in most of the rest of the world. Consequently, they will scarcely ever present the matter to their people. There are millions of Christians in this land who never read a missionary magazine and do not want to hear of missions. But be certain of this: thousands of millions of lost men and women will one day look us in the face in judgment, and God will ask, "Who failed to deliver these that were drawn unto death?" And the guilty will be without excuse.

We face a solemn accountability

"Shall not [God] render to every man according to his works?" Christian, you can do as you please now. God gives to everyone of us a strange and awful freedom to do as we like. Calmly the years go on, and no thunderbolts strike us down as we live in our selfishness and ease, spending our lives and means upon ourselves.

Recall how in Pilate's judgment hall the Master let the soldiers do their worst to Him. The chief priests and the other religious leaders carried the day: the time-serving governor condemned Jesus to death despite His innocence. They had their victory—then. But long since they have discovered their folly. What they did to Jesus has returned on their own wretched heads.

You can be selfish if you want. You can spend your

money as you please. But God is pondering your heart. He is weighing your life and calmly waiting until you are through revealing all that is in your heart. And then, oh, then!

I see two men passing into the judgment. One has spent his life for God. His money has been invested in immortal people. Hundreds meet him yonder as the fruit of his life. How he exults that he did not throw away this glorious crown and recompense!

But another comes. He has had the same means and the same opportunity. But he meets a blank eternity. There is no ransomed person to greet him. He has nothing to show for his life. His money is gone; he spent it on himself. And I think I see God taking him aside, pointing to the glorious scene that has greeted the other man. "My child," the Father says, "all that you see might have been your reward, too. It was waiting for you to claim. But you deprived yourself of it by your selfishness and neglect. Not only have you destroyed your own reward, but you have also destroyed all that company of immortal people whom you might have saved. Let the cries of those whom you have ruined be your sufficient punishment!"

There is a day of judgment now

But all the reckoning is not future. There is a day of judgment now. The word *pondereth* in Proverbs 24:12 literally means to weigh. God is weighing us, testing us according to how we meet His claims. He is determining by our present lives what we are fit for and can be trusted with. When God gives us money, He stands back and watches to see what we will do with it. If He discovers that we are good stewards, He entrusts us with more. If He sees that we are stingy, selfish persons, it is unlikely that He will give us a higher trust.

Even as you read these lines, God is pondering your heart and marking your very thoughts, purposes, excuses. The Scriptures ask, "What is man, that thou shouldest magnify him? and that thou shouldest set thine heart upon him? and that thou shouldest visit him every morning, and try him every moment?" (Job 7:17–18). How disappointed must God be when He finds us unworthy of His confidence and unfit to be trusted with the great things He would love to have us do for His kingdom! Many a business failure, many an earthly sorrow has come because we proved ourselves unworthy of God's great trust. On the other hand, many a fortune has been contributed to the cause of missions because some person was found on whom God could depend to be faithful in his or her stewardship.

"He that keepeth thy soul, doth not he know it?" We are dependent on God for our very lives and every blessing we have. How dare we ask God for anything when we know that even now He is looking into the face of some poor woman dying without the gospel whom we might have saved?

God feels the despair

And do you realize what else is happening every time you bow at His feet in prayer and expect Him to meet you with such gentleness and peace? God's heart is being wrung by the despairing cry of someone of His lost children who might have known His love if you had been faithful. I should be ashamed to pray to God tonight for His blessing on my head unless I believed that I was doing all in my power to send the gospel to a dying world. All of this we may not realize now, but the day is fast approaching when we shall come face to face with those who have perished without our assistance.

A missionary to Africa tells of a river village where he witnessed for a day. The people were bitterly disappointed when he told them he could not remain or leave an evangelist with them. They entreated him to change his plans, but it was beyond his power. Sorrowfully he cast off the moorings and pointed his boat upstream, the villagers still pleading and beckoning.

Two days later he returned downstream. As he approached the village where he had witnessed, people on the bank were watching. When they saw that he did not intend to land, they became wild in their gesticulations and cries, waving their arms, leaping high in the air, shouting and trying desperately to attract his attention. In every fiber of his being he felt their appeal, but he could do nothing. When at length the boat was out of sight of the villagers, the missionary said he heard a great and bitter cry go up from the people. It was a cry that seemed to reach heaven protesting to God the cruelty of man. It was the lamentation of lost people seeking after God.

You and I will hear that cry, for it will ring in our ears once more on the judgment day. What shall we do about it now? Will we be able to stand in that awful hour and declare with Paul, "I am pure from the blood of all men"?

We bear a responsibility

I have entitled this chapter "Christianity's Crime." You are not responsible for Christianity's crime, but you are responsible for all that you can do. The day has passed when missionary work can be done by great corporations or large organizations. God is going to do His best work by faithful individuals and often by humble instrumentalities. The few and not the many, the weak and not the great, the lowly and not the illustrious. It will be the little band, like Gideon's, picked out from a chosen people, that accomplishes God's will.

What can you do? Perhaps you can go, and go you should, unless God gives you a clearer call to stay. Perhaps you can support fully or partially someone who has gone or is going.

In Kansas I met a young man whom God had called to go to Africa. Along with him was a young farmer, a neighbor of the missionary under appointment. He, too, had wanted to go as a missionary. But with great sweetness he said to me, "I have wished very much to go as a missionary, but of late I think God is calling me to stay at home and support John while he is abroad." Those two men are joining hands across the waters. One is going to West Africa. The other, perhaps at equal or greater sacrifice, is staying at home. But by his hard toil and loving hands, he is backing up the first in his life work.

God is waiting to recruit an army of 20,000 heroes to go abroad and 20,000 more to "stay by the stuff" at home. And when the crowning day comes, they shall both divide the spoil.

What do you intend to do about this matter? Will you waste your money longer in the miserable investments which are to perish with this earth? Or are you going to turn your life into the currency of heaven and find it over yonder in immortal lives who will shine like stars forever in your crown of rejoicing?

In a very few years that world of people whom God expects you to save will all be dead and lost. The harvest will not wait. If the gospel is ever to be given to this generation, it must be done at once.

6

Twenty-one Reasons

WHAT SEVEN REASONS DO MANY PLEAD for neglecting the work of foreign missions? What are the seven *real* reasons for their negligence? And what are the seven reasons why we should make missions the supreme business of our lives?

The Bible calls our dedication to God a "reasonable service" (Romans 12:1). But many of God's sons and daughters find excuses to free themselves from this "reasonable service" that God has asked us to perform for Him.

Seven reasons we plead for neglecting missions

I call them reasons, but that is too good a term for them. In reality they are excuses. Here they are:

1. *What? Evangelize our political enemies?* It was Jonah's reason for resisting God's call to Nineveh, and it is the oldest excuse we find in the Bible for refusing to obey God's missionary mandate. Jonah tried to beg off because of his national and religious selfishness. He did not want Nineveh to be blessed or the godless in that city saved. Nineveh was Israel's political enemy, and Jonah was a patriotic Jew.

When at last God compelled Jonah to go and then

blessed his ministry beyond all precedent, Jonah became so angry that God had to leave him under his withered gourd as a warning to future generations against selfishness, bigotry and exclusivism.

2. *God must evangelize the nations.* In the era of modern church history this was the oldest excuse for neglecting missions. When a young lay minister in England proposed to a group of fellow ministers that they consider "means for converting the heathen," one of them retorted, "Young man, sit down. When God pleases to convert the heathen, He will do it without your aid or mine." But William Carey, divinely awakened to his biblical obligation, refused to be silenced. And the era of modern missions began.

3. *There is enough to do at home.* This old plea is really a pretext. In fact, those doing most for missions are doing most for the work at home. And those who beg off from foreign missions are as ready to be excused when the offering basket is passed for home work.

So obvious was this to a shrewd solicitor for city mission work in London that whenever he asked his wealthy constituency to donate to home missions he always wisely began with foreign missions. When they turned him down, remarking that there was plenty of work to do at home, he quickly brought out his other subscription book, which he had meant from the beginning to present. "I am so pleased," he would say, "to learn of your deep interest in home mission work. I have also brought along with me a report of our city mission. It will give me great pleasure to accommodate you in your preference for home missions."

4. One of the most common but saddest salves for guilty consciences is universalism—the unbiblical be-

lief that *God is too merciful to let anyone perish just because we neglect to take the gospel to him or her.* These like to call themselves liberal Christians. They insist that there really is salvation apart from the cross and God's plan of redemption.

Such a view is an insult to the precious blood of Jesus Christ and His demonstrated love for a lost world. If any less costly way of saving people could have sufficed, God would never have allowed His only begotten Son to be crucified. Verily, "there is none other name under heaven given among men, whereby we must be saved" (Acts 4:12).

5. *The non-Christian religions have much good in them.* This very popular plea has sprung from modern culture and the study of Oriental religions. Buddhism has been called "The Light of Asia." Confucianism has been praised for its high code of ethics. Hinduism has been actually imported into this country by weak and ignorant Americans who claim it a more ancient and profound system of spiritual truth than what the Bible sets forth.

It is necessary only to point to the lands where these religious systems have left their impress for thousands of years. What has Buddhism done for Tibet, its greatest stronghold? What has Hinduism done for India with its enslaving bonds of caste and superstition? What of China, notwithstanding its moral teaching? As for Islam, can we find a better proof of its blighting curse than in the troubled Middle East? When we look at parts of Africa, Polynesia and other barbarous and pagan lands, let the tragic story of the witch doctor and his victims and all the horrors of slavery and cannibalism be the test.

6. *Those overseas are not worth saving.* Even in our

enlightened day, some look upon the non-Caucasians abroad as stupid, ignorant, brutal — the offscouring of society. These suppose it might be better to leave them to their inevitable fate, to be swept away from the stronger tides of human life — a sort of spiritual survival of the fittest. Such is the argument of many insensitive, selfish men and women today. The non-Christians are not worth saving, goes the argument. Let them die out as inferior races.

Not worth saving? Then why did Jesus tell the story of the prodigal's welcome? Not worth saving? Then why did Jesus minister to the Syrophenician woman whose daughter was in need? Not worth saving? Then why did Jesus save the dying thief on the other cross? How can you explain the noble martyrs of China's Boxer Rebellion, the splendid trophies of Christian missions in Central Africa and Polynesia, the godly men and women who adorn the churches of Latin America today?

We ourselves would have been barbarians still had not Christian missionaries found our fathers and brought them to Christ Jesus the Light. They were wild Celts, Britons, Goths, Vandals, worshiping at the bloody altars of paganism and offering their very children in human sacrifice.

7. *We can't afford foreign missions.* Of all excuses parading in the guise of reasons, that is the meanest. Can it be that we cannot return to God, who gave us all we have, a small acknowledgement of His bounty to us? Is it possible we cannot trust the Lord of all the worlds and all wealth to make up to us what we put into His gracious hands?

When God's ancient people were faithful in giving to Him, they were doubly prosperous. It was only

when they were too stingy to give God the Sabbath
year that they lost what they foolishly tried to hoard.
How quickly Israel forgot that it was the Lord God
who gave "power to get wealth." How quickly *we*
forget.

Seven *real* reasons why we neglect missions

We have looked at seven reasons people plead for
neglecting missions. Each of the seven was an excuse,
not a reason. We turn from that trifling line of
thought to look at the real reasons why people neglect
the sacred trust Jesus Christ has left for us.

1. Undoubtedly the foremost reason why world
evangelization is so little considered is that *pastors do
not urge it*. They fail to press this matter upon their
congregations. The blood of the perishing multitudes
is on the hands of our pastors. Blindly and foolishly
considering only their local church interests, they
have lost the strength and support God would have
given them had they been faithful in this great trust. It
is an appalling fact that thousands of churches in
America contribute not a single dollar for the evangelization of the world. This is as foolish and blind as
it is sinful and negligent.

2. The second reason why Christians fail to work
for foreign missions is *ignorance—a lack of information
about the subject*. Bishop Taylor Smith of England has
said that the three things the church needs for a revival of missionary endeavor are "to know, to glow
and to go." We need to know God's plan for His
church in this age. How ignorant most Christians are
concerning it! We need to know the needs of our
perishing fellow beings and the fearful conditions
under which they live.

You would have no business pleading ignorance if your neighbor next door were slowly dying of cancer. You should know. And we need to know the facts concerning missions: the sacrifices and achievements, the stories of those who have suffered and labored and left us inspiring examples to urge us on in their footsteps. Do you know these things? Do you try to know them? Do you read about them? Do you love to hear of them? Do you subscribe to a missionary periodical and read its stirring pages with interest and delight?

3. The most general cause of missionary indifference is *a low spiritual life*. Barely saved, multitudes of Christians squeeze through life with just enough religion to get by. They want to hang onto the world and get as much out of it as they can.

The secret of missionary enthusiasm is a heart consecrated to God and a Spirit-filled life. Until Christ gets His true place in the center of our being we will be good neither for missions or for any other Christian work. Therefore, in our conventions our first work is to get God's children wholly yielded to Him in practical consecration. We must see that they are filled with Christ and fired with the spirit of love and power. Without those credentials, we are not going to take any practical interest in the message of missions.

If need be, repent of your selfishness and worldliness. Give God the life He redeemed and claims. Then let Him give back to you power and love and a willingness for service and, with these, His own exceedingly great reward.

4. The fourth real reason why people neglect missions is their *worldliness and self-indulgence*. Christians today are increasingly given to pleasure and extravagance. There has been a great increase of wealth in our

land, but no such proportionate increase in giving to God. Where does the money go? It goes to the theater, the summer outings, the automobiles. It goes to home furnishings, to clothing, to travel, to an affluent lifestyle as we transfer more and more things from the luxury category to necessities.

Do a little calculating. Add up what you have paid in the past 12 months for clothing, amusements, recreation, light reading, home furnishings. Put that sum against the amount of your most recent faith promise for missions. How do the two compare? Must you be ashamed at how relatively little you give for missions?

5. Just as bad as material selfishness is our *religious selfishness*—another reason for our neglect of world evangelization. We spend great sums on the architecture and adorning of our churches. Motivated largely by denominational pride, we multiply our churches. We must have the best in music. We support higher education. We want the pleasure of going to seminars and conventions for spiritual help. Compare those sums with what you give for the spiritually perishing. How does it look? How does it look in *God's* sight?

6. A sixth reason for neglecting missions is our *lack of training in scriptural giving*. Very few Christians really know how to give to God. Giving is like a taste for certain food; once acquired, it can become intense.

In His Word God has given us a simple plan. In essence, we are to lay by us systematically according to how much God has prospered us. What we thus set aside is God's and must be used faithfully in His service. The advantage is that we have a certain fund that is absolutely for religious purpose. The only question still to determine is what proportion will go for each particular object. The money is there; it just needs sound judgment to divide it justly and fairly between the various interests concerned.

Suppose, for example, you have $100.00 of the Lord's money. Instead of giving it all to the church organ fund or even to your minister's salary, you need to make a fair distribution. God's perishing lambs on the dark mountains of earth should not be forgotten in the distribution.

Why not estimate your probable income for the next 12 months? Whether it is $1,000 from a part-time job or $50,000 or more, the very least you should think of giving to God is one tenth. That was ancient benevolence and, in fact, less than the nearly three tenths that Israel returned to God. With God's portion thus determined, suppose you give half of it to God's work at home and the other half to the immensely vaster field and greater need abroad.

But you are not through yet. That is the tithe. Now pray and ask God how much more you may dare to add in faith. There may be some unknown sources of income that you can trust God for. I should not be surprised if you doubled what you initially set aside for God.

But reflect once more. Bow your head and ask God how much more you can add to the sum by real sacrifice in the next 12 months. If this works with you as it has with many others, the total could leap by 400 percent or more. And that is God's method of Christian giving: a fair proportion stretched to a much larger proportion by faith and loving sacrifice.

7. The last reason for neglecting missions mingles with all the others and helps to explain them. It is the *lack of true love for Christ*. If you have a great love in your heart for anyone, it will stop at nothing. It will

overcome any obstacle. It will find a way through any combination of difficulties.

If you have no love for Christ in your heart, everything will seem difficult and insurmountable. Stop working for the church or for missions and start working for Christ. See that thorn-crowned head. Hear that one name above every name. Listen to Jesus' plea: "Lovest thou Me?" Let the love of Christ constrain you, and missions will not be neglected.

Seven reasons why missions should be our supreme business

We hasten to consider seven reasons for making missions our one overriding objective. Here they are:

1. World evangelization is our *duty*. "I am debtor" is the terse, practical way in which Paul summed it all up. Missions is not a sentiment, not a notion, not a fad. It is a debt — a matter of common honesty.

Missions is a debt because the gospel has been committed to us as a trust, not as a personal luxury. Our Master has commanded us to give the gospel to all the world. Someone brought the good news to our forefathers. Now we owe it to other races to pass it on to them. It is the supreme duty of every Christian to give to every being in the present generation an opportunity to be saved. Not to do so is the crime of Christianity, the unpardonable sin of the church of Christ. It is the sin of breach of trust. It is the sin of disobedience to the Lord's last command. It is the sin of spiritual murder and blood-guilt. Is it *your* sin?

2. *Compassion* is the next reason for making missions our supreme business. The condition of those who have not Christ is utterly hopeless, sad, despairing. There is no such equal condition in our home-

land. There is no one here but can hear of Christ in some way.

How different it is in most of the overseas lands. The things we hold dear they do not have: our precious Bible, our beloved church fellowship, the Christian day in seven for worship and rest, peace through the blood of Christ, the sweet hope of heaven above. Think of Sunday school with its hallowed associations of childhood. Think of deathbeds where father, mother, wife, husband, children have passed through the valley of the shadow to a living, eternal hope. All of this is utterly unknown where the gospel has not taken root. What right do we have to keep these blessings to ourselves?

But add this besides: the horrors of slavery, of opium addiction, of witch doctors, of child widows, of cruel pagan rites. How can we dare tell our Master there is nothing we can do to brighten that black picture and save those perishing ones?

3. A third reason for making missions our supreme business is the *results* we see. Missionary statistics confirm that the rate of conversions overseas are many times greater than they are in our average church at home. To be sure, there are resistant areas where conversions are few. But speaking generally, there is no Christian work in which a little enterprise, a little seed sowing so quickly blossoms into a mighty harvest.

4. *God is mightily working in many overseas lands*, and this is a summons for us to be workers together with Him. Isaiah heard the heavenly seraphim say of Jehovah, "The whole earth is full of his glory" (Isaiah 6:3). If that were true 3,000 years ago when only one nation knew Jehovah God, is it less true today?

The New Testament speaks of angels being "ministering spirits, sent forth to minister for them who shall be heirs of salvation" (Hebrews 1:14). They minister not only to the actual heirs of salvation but for those who "shall be heirs." They are ministering today for many people who shall yet be heirs of salvation, bringing light to the darkness, bringing those who dwell in darkness to the light.

Our Almighty God is converging His forces in earth's darkest lands. Every year has witnessed miracles of Providence in every corner of the globe. Roads and railroads have opened remote areas to the gospel of Christ. And at the same time the Holy Spirit has been poured out as never before upon all flesh. China is one continuous miracle—a sort of living picture on an endless chain of new wonders. Korea has passed through a mighty revival. Missionaries report many accessions to the churches of Christ in thousands of mission stations around the globe. God is pouring floods upon the dry ground and the latter rain is falling. Surely we should be working with God when He Himself is so mightily marching on.

5. *Missionary work will hasten the personal return of the Lord Jesus Christ.* The worldwide preaching of the gospel appears to be the one yet unfulfilled condition in preparation for His return. It marks on the dial of the ages the hour when the clock of destiny will strike, sounding the knell of the old dispensation and the advent of the new. Jesus promised, "This gospel of the kingdom shall be preached in all the world for a witness unto all nations; and then shall the end come" (Matthew 24:14). If we would be in line with the providence and purposes of God, the line that leads to the marriage supper of the Lamb and the kingdom of

our God and His Christ, let us be and do our best for the immediate evangelization of the world.

6. *Our love for Christ should impel us to pursue the missionary task that is close to His heart.* We have already seen that the lack of love for Christ is the cause of unfaithfulness in world evangelization. Only love can inspire and sustain a true and lasting missionary zeal. Once more, let all other attractions pass; let us see no one save Jesus only. He is the Man of Macedonia crying, "Come over and help us." He is the sad Shepherd looking upon a perishing world and plaintively asking, "Lovest thou me more than these? Feed my lambs. . . . Feed my sheep" (John 21:15–16).

You were lost, and He loved and sought out you. By that love and by all that Jesus' cross and precious blood have ever meant to you, go forth to seek and save the lost. Will you respond to the Master's unequivocal command, "Go ye into all the world, and preach the gospel to every creature"?

7. Finally, *the blessings that come through missionary outreach* should make world evangelization our supreme object. There is but one way to be a happy, triumphant Christian. That is to live out the cross of Christ, to give forth the love, the grace and the great salvation Christ has given us.

If Christ were on earth today, His willing feet would go to these dark, lost lands. If Christ were here today, His hands would be stretched out to the perishing as they were stretched out on earth to the suffering and the lost. If Christ were here today, His voice would cry once more in the ears of all the weary and the burdened, "Come unto me, all ye that labour and are heavy laden, and I will give you rest" (Matthew 11:28).

But Christ is not on earth today in literal flesh and blood. He has passed within the heavenly gates, where His hands and voice are lifted in intercession before the throne for us. Therefore, He asks for our hands, our feet, our voices.

Will you be feet for Him to go up the mountains of darkness and sin? Will you be hands for Him to feed the perishing multitudes for whom His heart is moved with compassion? Will you be a tongue for Him to tell of His love, His mercy and His precious salvation? Will you take the cross that has redeemed you and pass it on to your perishing brothers and sisters overseas? Will you take the cup of salvation that has quenched your burning thirst and hand it to the famishing children of a lost world?

Will you lay up in store this mighty recompense that Christ has promised? "Inasmuch as ye have done it unto one of the least of these my brethren, ye have done it unto me."

CHAPTER
7

The Heart of Missions

WITHOUT A DOUBT, THE GREATEST text in the Bible is John 3:16: "For God so loved the world, that he gave his only begotten Son, that whosoever believeth in him should not perish, but have everlasting life."

This statement by our Lord is so transcendentally greater than the highest human thought that I shrink from even trying to discuss it. To many it has been a message of salvation, bringing them to saving faith in Jesus Christ. I want to look at it here as a missionary message. In this statement I see three plain and emphatic thoughts:

1. This is the God the world needs to know.
2. This is the gospel the world needs to hear.
3. This is the love the world needs to see.

The platform of missions is (a) a God of love, (b) the good news about Christ our Savior and (c) God's love within us sacrificing, serving, sending, going, praying. May God give you and me the love that will involve us in His great plan.

The God the world needs to know

The unregenerate world does not lack for gods. It has many gods. The devil has taken pains to see to that. He has provided mankind with abundant religious privileges. He loves to play God himself and to be the counterfeit of our heavenly Father. In every land and tribe he has his priesthood and rites.

From earliest times we find evidences of worship among all peoples. The ancient Egyptians had deities that were gross, absurd, revolting. Bugs, beetles, serpents, repulsive crawling things were the objects of their compulsory obeisance. Their mythology teems with pictures of the future world at once ridiculous, revolting and terrible. They knew something of justice in the heavenly world and the awards of the future life, but they knew nothing of love and grace.

The deities of the Phoenicians and the Sidonians — Baal and Ashteroth — were the vilest of representations. Their worship was an orgy of abominable sensuality. And something more hideous could scarcely be produced than the god of the Moabites and the Ammonites — that frightful Molech, worshiped by the human sacrifices of helpless little children. The statue was a great brazen furnace heated red hot with burning coals. Innocent children were cradled in Molech's fiery arms while loud music drowned their fearful screams. Even Solomon set up a shrine of Molech on one of the heights overlooking Jerusalem.

What shall we say of the mythology of the Greeks and the Romans? Their religions were but the perpetuations of human passions and vices. What was Venus but the impersonation of lust? What was Jupiter but a type of the despotic power which Nero and Domitian exercised? As we progress through the ages we find our Druid forefathers offering human sacrifices. In parts of Africa and in other areas yet today we find fetish worship in which the lowest and most senseless things are set apart as deities. Go throughout China and you will see in their images the same kind of revolting worship and the cruelest of traditions in connection with the future punishment of the dead. Until the evangels of Christ introduced it, they had no word for love. They had no word for sin. To them their gods were representations of the human heart, and "they that make them are like unto them" (Psalm 115:8).

How different the God Jesus showed us

When we turn to the picture Jesus gives us of God, how holy, how attractive He is! God is one, God is pure. God is infinitely merciful, gentle, compassionate. And God is near. He is at the side of His suffering children. He is there to meet our needs, speak to our hearts, to be our Comforter, our Friend. Not even the faintest approximation of this sublime picture is to be found in any human religions. We may find some shadow of the unity of God in Islam, some suggestion of His omnipresence in pantheism, but how cold and hard and comfortless when compared with the genuine!

It was Jesus who gave us the God who is at once just and merciful, holy and beneficent, majestic and yet "our Father who art in heaven." The non-Christian world has no such God. And it is our business to tell a groping, searching world of our God, our Father, our King of love.

So this is the first message that the Father has for us

to tell. Tell the world of your God, for it has no such God. At best it has the unknown God. Terrifying things it worships. Its religions are the sources of its most fearful suffering. Shall we go to our world and tell it of our God? Shall we give to the world our God and the love that will make Him as real to the people of our world as He has been to us?

The gospel the world needs to hear

This gospel of John 3:16 is what the world needs to hear. It is the gospel of "whosoever will." It is the gospel of everlasting love. It is the gospel of full and free salvation through Jesus Christ our Lord. The word *gospel* means "good news," "glad tidings."

Turn to the joyless faces of those who know not Christ Jesus, and you have an object lesson describing the devil's religions. My most profound impression in my travels abroad has been the passive misery stamped on the faces of the myriads who tramp in monotonous despair from cradle to grave. There are no glad tidings. There is no happy girlhood or boyhood. There is no joyful, radiant beauty. There is only darkness and despair.

India alone has innumerable gods—one for nearly every inhabitant. How degrading, how unsatisfying, how repulsive they are with their splashes of red. Brahmanism and the caste system it has produced condemns men and women to hopeless despair. They cannot rise above their present level. And in the world to come their only prospect is a progressive reincarnation from insect to beast to possibly being reborn a man in some remote future age.

Buddhism is a dream: ignore your misery, cease to recognize it and you will not see its evil. Retire to the inward calm of your heart as you strive for Nirvana, the cessation of existence. It may be comfortable for a dirty fat priest who has everything he wants. But for the crushed, brokenhearted votary, there is no life, no hope. Confucianism is a system of morals, of culture. It teaches obedience to parents, but it knows nothing of God. It will help a person as long as he or she does right, but when the person falls it has no arm reaching out to help.

Islam is consecrated lust and lies. Its fearful shadow has fallen over great portions of our world. It conquers by the sword, not by love. It does not liberate; it enslaves. Judaism is Christianity's scaffolding. Those who embrace it suppose they have the temple when, in reality, they have only the pipes and the planks used in its construction. Judaism leads up to Christianity. It tells people what they ought to do. But it does not enable them to do it.

Spiritism counterfeits the Holy Spirit. It misleads its followers into foolishly worshiping the very devil himself. As for materialism, the religion of our own culture, the philosopher Herbert Spencer, in a letter to a friend shortly before his death, best expressed its emptiness: "I may not see another springtime. All I can say is that I have this conviction left . . . that somewhere in this universe there is a force of some kind that is moving things, but it is all blind and dark to me. My philosophy gives me no consolation as I look into my own grave."

A great contrast

With few exceptions, the religions of the world have no ideals or morals, no high standards of goodness and righteousness, no spirituality, no unpolluted conduct and character, no pattern to lift us. Read the mythology of Vishnu, the popular god of India. It is the tale of a vile, sensual wretch. The worst thing about sin is that the sinner cannot by himself or herself be good. Some ask, Will not God be merciful to those who do the best they know to do? The fact is, they have no power to obey their consciences. Jesus Christ gives us power to be good, power to rise above sin. That is salvation.

Apart from Christ there is no power, no Holy Spirit, no love. Therefore, there is no remedy for the guilty conscience. There is no provision for the deep sense of sin. All know that sense of sin, but they have no answer for a guilty conscience. They go down to death in eternal despair with their sins upon their heads. They know about their sins and they know they are lost. They have no hope for the future, no bright heaven, no waiting loved ones to greet them there. They have only darkness and uncertainty.

Someone remarked, "The difference between Christian and other lands is that people do wrong in Christian lands in spite of their religion; people do wrong in other lands in the name of their religion." The statement is generally true. *We* may be wicked contrary to what our mothers and fathers taught us; *they* are apt to be wicked because their parents and priests and religions taught them to be so.

Such is the contrast between "religions" and the gospel of Jesus Christ. The good news we have is that "whosoever believeth in [God's only begotten Son, Jesus Christ] shall not perish, but have everlasting life." Ours is a salvation that meets our eternal need and opens the gates of heaven. It is a salvation that answers to our consciences, answers to the claims of

God, answers to the demands of the law. It tells us that God's holiness has been satisfied. It makes being good as natural as once it was natural to be bad. It brings the omnipotence of God into our hearts and lives, causing us to do right. God declares: "I will put my spirit within you, and cause you to walk in my statutes, and ye shall keep my judgments, and do them" (Ezekiel 36:27).

The gospel of Christ opens to us the gates of heaven. We may walk in the light of the city. We may talk to our heavenly Father. We know where our departed believing loved ones have gone, and we can look forward to joining them in bliss no human poetry or imagination ever dreamed of.

Jesus Christ remedies the wrongs of society not by making society good but by making individual people good. He reforms society by reforming its individual members. And He will not cease until He has banished all evils from this globe and

> He shall make this blighted earth
> His own fair world again.

The love the world needs to see

"God so loved . . . that he gave." "God . . . gave his only begotten Son." God gave His best. He gave His best to unworthy men and women. He gave the world His best because He loved the world. And if we are to give Christ to the world, it will be because we also love the world.

The world needs our love. An American corporation can write the names of its products on the rocks of the Himalayas (I have seen them emblazoned there), but God does not write His gospel on rocks or in the sky. He wants a sympathetic medium. He wants a person who has been touched by that gospel — a person who can communicate His love to others. It is possible to shape a piece of ice into a magnifying glass that will converge the rays of the sun to start a fire. But God does not kindle hearts that way. In the communication of the gospel, the medium must be aflame with God's love before that love can be communicated.

So God waits. He waits for us to so love and to so go. God could have sent a thousand angels. He could have written His gospel on the stars. Instead, He has entrusted its communication to us. Some years ago I visited one of our missionaries in China. As we walked down the street, a man nodded to him. "We have lived here now for five years," the missionary said to me, "and this year is the first that people have even looked at us. They thought we had come for some selfish purpose. Now they can see that we love them. They believe in our unselfish purpose. They now speak to us, and they are beginning to listen to our gospel."

I heard about a little fellow who was hospitalized. Good people stopped by to say nice things to him and even leave him some flowers. But he had a boy's heart, and a boy's stomach. "They talk a lot about love, but I would like to see a little of it," he commented. The next day someone brought him fruit to eat, and then he could understand their love. So it is with the world of lost mankind. People need to see our love demonstrated, and then they will understand the love of our God.

God wants to put His own love in us and make it a passion, a delight and a necessity of our nature to bless others. When Christ comes into our hearts, this happens. Communicating the gospel of Christ to others should become the first business of our lives.

Letting John 3:16 come alive

One of the bright Christian women of our day, who heads a great school that has sent out many missionaries, told a group of young people how John 3:16 had gripped her. "I determined to devote an evening to the text until it took hold of me. I got no further than 'God so loved.' The thought grew so big and glorious that it filled my soul. I wrote the words in my diary, underlined them and covered them with my tears."

She said she returned to the text weeks later and spent an evening on the next three words: "that he gave." As she meditated she wrote:

God so loved that He gave.
I so love that I give—

"And there," she added, "I left a blank, and God talked to me. He said, 'Gave *what?*' I thought, *God gave His best, His all, His only begotten Son.* Then I wrote in that blank, 'I so love that I give my best, my all'."

That is what this text means. And the challenge comes likewise to you and to me. Will you take that blank and fill it in with a precious love gift to God? It is so easy to give when we love!

One Christmas in West Africa, a missionary asked the African girls to bring an offering for Jesus. Each brought some little thing—a flower or some toy she had been given by passing traders. But one girl with deep-set eyes and a face transfigured, handed the missionary a little bundle. When he had opened it, he discovered the equivalent of 85 cents. For a poor girl in West Africa at that time, it was a small fortune.

The missionary called the girl over. "My child," he asked, "how could you do this?"

"Jesus gave Himself for me," she replied, "and I thought I would give myself for Him. I sold myself for the rest of my life to a planter. I gave him the right to use me in his field at the hardest toil, and he gave me 85 cents and let me have this one day so I could bring the money to you."

The missionary was overwhelmed. Sixty years of drudgery, of unrequited toil in the burning fields of Africa with no freedom. The girl might never love anyone for herself or have anything of her own. Her whole life was mortgaged to a planter so that she might have 85 cents to give to Jesus Christ.

That is what God's love can do. Let the sacrifice of that humble girl speak to you. Let it influence your heart. Let it become a passion in your soul. When that happens, God will see the travail of His Son's soul and be satisfied.

How can we love like God loved?

A very practical question arises: What if the people God wants us to love are unlovable—even repulsive? How can we love people we do not like?

We can love them because they are dear to God. God cares for them. Do you remember the story of the boy who knocked on the door of a farmhouse in Illinois? The farmer and his wife were about to turn him away, saying they had no place for tramps. But with trembling hands the young man pulled out a scraggly looking piece of paper and handed it to the couple. The handwriting was that of their son, who had been killed in battle. "Dear Father and Mother," the note began, "The bearer of this letter is my friend. He has been waiting on me, helping me as I grow weaker from my wounds. If I don't get home, love him for my sake. Tom." I tell you, that mother's arms flew open and that father's tears began to flow. The "tramp" became a son for Tom's sake.

Today Jesus presents to us a world of sad-faced, brokenhearted, hopeless people. "I loved them," He says, "enough to die for them. They are dear to me. I died for you when you were no better. Love them for my sake."

The poet Montgomery tells of meeting a stranger who asked him for help. As he gave it, it seemed as if he himself was restored and all his own wounds were healed and his heart made glad. He wondered who the stranger could be.

> Then in a moment to my view
>   The stranger turned from his disguise.
> The tokens in His hands I knew;
>   My Savior stood before my eyes.
> He spoke, and my poor name He named,
> "Of Me thou hast not been ashamed;
> These deeds shall thy memorial be.
> Fear not, thou didst it unto Me."

Then, again, you can love the unlovely because they have the potential of being noble and good. When they become Christians they become glorious Christians. Think of the two Africans who stood so faithfully by David Livingstone during those long jungle treks. When Livingstone died, they carried his body in their arms through the swamps of Africa, through perils of wild beasts and wicked men, to the coast, where it could be shipped to England for burial in Westminster Abbey. That is how the African can love and sacrifice.

When Polhill Turner was sentenced to be beaten by the Chinese because he tried to go into Tibet, two Chinese instead bared their backs to the rods. Ten years afterward, their scars remained, but the two men counted it a great privilege to suffer for the cause of Jesus Christ. That is how the Chinese can love and sacrifice.

At the least, pity the lost

If we can love them no other way, let it be with the love of pity. They desperately need the compassion of Jesus Christ. Take a piece of paper and put on it two dots for every second. Keep it up for an hour and there will be 7,200 dots. In that hour *at least* that many people died without Christ in our dark, lost world. With every breath we breathe, people are perishing. Can you muster no loving concern for their plight?

A Chinese was seen on a mountainside where pilgrims went to worship. "What are you seeking?" they asked him. "I am trying to find the door of heaven," he replied. "I feel and feel and feel, but I cannot find it." Pitiful! ". . . if haply they might feel after [the Lord], and find him, though he be not far from every one of us" (Acts 17:27).

A missionary told of hearing a little lamb bleating pitifully in the night. She wished she could go to it, for she had heard also the jackals back in the mountains, and she knew the lamb would be an easy prey. The lamb continued to bleat, and the missionary found herself emotionally caught up in the drama. Suddenly, she said, she heard the shepherd's answering call. He had heard the lamb's cry, and he seemed to be reassuring the little creature, "I am coming. I am coming!" The poor little lamb got quiet and still because the shepherd had heard its cry.

Not lambs but human beings for whom Christ died are crying in the night. God heard their cry and in love sent His Son—that great Shepherd of the sheep. Will we, too, heed their cry for help and go in Jesus name?

The Grace of Giving

WHEN WE GIVE OUR BLESSINGS TO OTHERS, they return in double measure. If we have been experiencing the fullness of the Holy Spirit in our lives, we are glad for the opportunity to express our love to God and to our fellow beings. We hear the Master saying, "Freely ye have received, freely give" (Matthew 10:8).

A country's export trade must properly balance its import trade if it is to be economically viable. One reason for the extraordinary prosperity of the United States has been its historic ability to export more in dollar value than it has had to import from abroad. So in the Christian life, if we are to prosper spiritually we must "export" in service to others at least as much as we take in in blessing. Many are stalled in their Christian lives simply because they do not give out to others. They are stagnant pools.

Missions imparts unspeakable blessings. It does more for us than we do for those without Christ in foreign lands. Surely it is very important for us to note, from time to time, the biblical principles, motives and true methods of giving. Certainly no text is more appropriate than one Paul wrote to the Corinthians:

> For ye know the grace of our Lord Jesus Christ, that though he was rich, yet for your sakes he became poor, that ye through his poverty might be rich (2 Corinthians 8:9).

Seven ways of giving

Someone has remarked that there are seven ways of giving. There is the *careless* way—giving something to every appeal that comes along, perhaps just to get rid of the person making the request. There is the *impulsive* way—giving when you feel like it, when your emotions are stirred. There is the *lazy* way: finding someone who will get up a fair, a festival, an ice cream social and raising the money that way. (In the end, it is the most expensive way to give!) There is also the *selfish* way: giving to a project, such as a new church organ, or a person, perhaps the pastor, from which or whom the giver will personally benefit. I know of churches that spend more in a year on embellishments to their sanctuary than they give in a century to missions.

Then there is the *systematic* way of giving—setting aside a certain percent of your means—and I am glad to report that systematic giving is becoming more popular among intelligent Christians. There is also what we might call the *fair* way of giving—giving for the Lord's work as much as we spend on ourselves. Finally, there is the *heroic* way, the self-sacrificing way. This is giving until it hurts and then giving until it stops hurting. It is giving more than you can.

God has not left us without clear teaching on the

subject of Christian giving. Not surprisingly, giving is a major subject of the letters to the Corinthian church. More so than with most of Paul's other letters, these two were written to set forth the doctrine, regulate the discipline and determine the government of the Christian church. They are handbooks for the church of Jesus Christ throughout the Christian age. In them is almost all that we need to know regarding church polity. And giving is one of the subjects covered.

Giving is a grace God bestows

First, note in Second Corinthians 8 that giving is a grace God bestows. "We do you to wit [that is, we want you to know] of the grace of God bestowed on the churches of Macedonia" (verse 1). "See that ye abound in this grace also" (verse 7). Giving is not something we have to do. It is something God will do if we will let Him.

What is grace? Grace is something given us, something we get, not something we give. God does not require us to give as though it was a difficult exercise. He wants to give us the spirit of giving. Giving is something we must do in the power of the Holy Spirit. It is something we must take as a divine gift, a grace of the Holy Spirit. Therefore giving belongs to the essential qualities of holiness and right living. Without this grace we cannot call ourselves truly sanctified children of God. Thankfully, because it is a grace, it is available to each of us.

Giving is a privilege of the poor. The very poorest may give, and God will enable them to give. Giving is not for the wealthy, for the millionaire. It is for the humble and the poor, for those of the smallest resources and the most modest means. It was "in a great trial of affliction" and out of "deep poverty" that the Macedonians gave (verse 2). But the "abundance of their joy and their deep poverty abounded unto the riches of their liberality." God requires the poor to give because giving is a grace. It is God's doing, not man's. Therefore God chooses the weakest of the people to do it.

When God wanted to honor an Old Testament servant of His, He laid that servant's support upon a poor widow. He sent Elijah to an impoverished widow of Zarephath. She had but a handful of meal and a small amount of cooking oil. *Because* she was poor, God required of the widow that she undertake the support of His messenger. And her giving became God's grace. "The barrel of meal wasted not, neither did the cruse of oil fail, according to the word of the Lord, which he spake by Elijah" (1 Kings 17:16).

A New Testament example

Jesus commended above all others a poor widow who cast two mites into the Temple treasury. Because there was more love in the gift, more motive, more of God, it was the larger. It outweighed all the wealth that was poured into the treasury.

I heard of a minister who told a very humble congregation of saints that not one person among them — man, woman, child — was so poor but that he or she could give something to the Lord. One woman went home and had a good cry over the minister's remark. *I am so poor*, she thought, *I cannot give anything.* After she had wept for a while, the Lord began to talk to her. "You cannot give like other people," He said, "but you can give like a child. You can begin by putting aside a *penny.*" Do you know, when the year ended that impoverished woman had $21.00 to give! It was the largest single gift of anyone in the entire congregation of working people.

When we began our mission on Tremont Street in Boston, I remember taking up an offering for it at an afternoon meeting in the city. The largest gift was $25.00 — a substantial sum at that time. I was curious as to who the "$25.00 person" was. At the close of the meeting I was introduced to him — a poor shoemaker who had a small shop. When I spoke to him about his generous gift he said, "If you only knew what the Lord has given me, you would not wonder at all." Subsequently I became better acquainted with the man. Every time I went to Boston, there he was, shouting his hallelujahs. He was converted many years before, but He could get no joy. He was hungry for more of God's presence. He sought a deeper experience with God, but the members of the church he attended told him such a quest was nonsense. "You must be contented to sin like the rest of us," they advised.

The man backslid and for several years he kept a saloon in Boston. But his heart hunger would not go away. One Thursday afternoon he stumbled into our Alliance meeting in Boston and heard people telling about the riches of Christ's grace. Before the afternoon was over, he had received the Holy Spirit. He went home to pitch his whiskey into the sea. He closed his saloon and returned to making shoes for a living. There in his little shop he preached the gospel all day long to the customers.

And that was the man who gave the $25.00. It was a gift that God enabled and that God impelled by the fullness of the Holy Spirit and the overflow of His grace.

We can give beyond our power

In the next place, we can give beyond our power. If giving is a grace, it is always beyond our power. In the natural we cannot understand this. We are willing to go about holiness supernaturally, but when it comes to giving we go about it as a matter of business. God wants us to go about our giving as we go about our other blessings — by faith. Paul says of the Macedonians, "To their power, . . . yea, and beyond their power they were willing of themselves" (2 Corinthians 8:3). They gave more than they were able to give just because it was a grace.

Grace is what God can do, not what we can do. Give, believing that God can supply even more than you can see of resources and ability. Believe that He can save for you and enable you to do in this as in other things more than you could in yourself — even beyond your power.

But note that the giving of the Macedonians was voluntary. It was willing giving. They did not have to be pressed. In fact, they had to be held back. Paul says they urged their gifts upon him: "Praying us with much intreaty that we would receive the gift, and take upon us the fellowship of the ministering to the saints" (verse 4). They were like the children of Israel when the tabernacle was about to be built. Moses had to stop the offerings. That is God's standard of giving. Its secret? Personal consecration to God.

God first wants us

Personal consecration to God is the secret of voluntarily giving beyond our power. "They . . . first gave their own selves to the Lord, and unto us by the will of God" (verse 5). Once they had given themselves, it was easy to give anything and everything else. All true giving begins with consecration. I might talk to 10,000 ordinary people and not get a thousand dollars for missions. In fact, I would not attempt it unless the hearts of the people were prepared. I have witnessed meetings where thousands of people, representing millions of dollars of capital, gave only a few paltry dollars for world evangelization. I have also seen a poor, humble congregation give thousands of dollars for missions.

When our missionary offerings began to be reported in the sensational press, people often came to me to learn the secret. Agents from large organizations asked me what sort of hypnotism I used. Had I discovered a new auctioneering style? They would scarcely believe me when I told them we had no magnetism and used no manipulation. The secret of the large offerings was people so filled with the Holy Spirit and the joy of the Lord that they could not keep back anything from Christ Jesus.

When we truly give ourselves to the Lord, we give Him everything. Our clothes, our food, the support of our family—all of these are consecrated to the Lord. Holiness unto the Lord is written upon everything we do. It is not merely what a person puts in the offering plate. When the chords of self are cut, it is a joy to give everything to God.

There must also be loyalty to a cause

Let me call your attention to another point often overlooked. The Macedonians not only gave them-

selves to the Lord first, but they then gave themselves
to the special cause that Paul and his associate workers
represented — a missionary campaign. Note again
Paul's words, "They gave their own selves . . . unto us
by the will of God."

In the days of Israel's early monarchy, David's men
were of one heart to make him king. They were men
who knew their place, men who "kept rank," men
who were true to their fellow soldiers. The Lord Jesus
has not only called us to be true to Him, but in Him to
be true to our fellow workers. Then we can be de-
pended on. Then we will not lose our human concern.
In every great movement established to hasten the
return of the King and to further His cause, God
wants and expects this true touch of loyal service.

We are bound together in a fellowship that reaches
around the world. We stand heart to heart, shoulder to
shoulder and hand to hand in the great and solemn
trust God has committed to us. He has called us into it
and He expects us to be true to our trust as well as
true to Him. Only then can He make us "terrible as an
army with banners" in carrying out the great commission of world evangelization.

God in His providence continues to raise up spiritual movements. The Reformation was one. It was
because Luther and the Elector of Saxony and the
reforms in Switzerland, Scotland and England stood
shoulder to shoulder that they were able to give us the
Bible and the gospel. In the 17th and 18th centuries,
God was pleased to give us men like Whitefield, the
Wesleys and Doddridge. Through their union they
became a force for righteousness. They witnessed to
divine transactions that have become our heritage of
blessing yet today. They gathered around them spiri-

tual men and women who have become leaders in many a field of Christian testimony.

When God called me to know Him in His fullness, He was at the same time calling others into a similar experience of holiness and healing and a similar longing to take the whole gospel to the whole world. Humans were not marshalling this army. The living God was doing so. It is not my cause, it is God's cause. It is a special movement that has arisen out of special conditions. I will lose my blessing if I grow careless, lukewarm or faithless to this trust. God holds me true to the Word that has blessed me and true to the world that needs me. And He wants to hold you true to the Word and the world, too.

A double consecration

Do remember this double consecration: First, give yourself to God and then give yourself in fellowship with your brothers and sisters in Christ to the great cause of witnessing for Him. Do it in His fullness, giving the gospel to the present generation even to the uttermost parts of earth.

There are millions of Christians who will do the other things that need to be done. They will work for social reform, for educational achievement, for political goals. All of these have their place. But if God has given you something better, He gave it to you that you might pass it on to others. And He holds you responsible to that sacred trust. Hundreds of missionaries in perilous places belong to you. They expect you to stand true to them.

I believe God wants a spirit of magnificent loyalty to possess us in these days. Our missionary colaborers work bravely through summer heat and winter cold, in physical danger and amid spiritual pressures. They belong to us by love, by prayer, by sacrifice, by everything in our power. God will hold us responsible to stand with them. If we get careless and let some little trifle chill our faithfulness and zeal, their blood will some day rest upon our heads.

The missionary faith offering

Finally, Second Corinthians 8 provides light on the practice of missionary faith offerings. Have we scriptural warrant for making an estimate of what we will give in the coming year for the cause of missions? Must we simply give as we are able and make no firm commitment? Is the pledging system scriptural?

I am glad to say I find it right in this chapter. Paul says: "This is expedient for you, who have begun before, not only to do, but also to be forward a year ago" (verse 10). In chapter 9, verse 2, the apostle continues: "I know the forwardness of your mind, for which I boast of you to them of Macedonia, that Achaia was ready a year ago; and your zeal hath provoked very many." Paul is saying they made their commitments in advance. They did it in meekness and gentleness of spirit, and the news went abroad through the churches. It reached Macedonia, and the Macedonians were inspired to do likewise. It encouraged many of them, and it was a blessing even before a single cent was paid. The pledging was a blessing, and it was undoubtedly acceptable to God. He was pleased with their planning.

God is still pleased when we plan our giving. As we review our mercies and blessings, as we look out upon a world in need of Christ Jesus, we can determine that by God's help we will give x amount in the next 12 months for the spread of the gospel. This is not pledged as a promissory note. It is a covenant between us and God. It is simply an endeavor on our part—just like what the Corinthians were doing.

When we commit ourselves in this way, it gives us something to live for. It helps us to take Christ into partnership in our businesses. It motivates us to sacrifice and save. It is a goal to live up to, and it has an uplifting, inspiring influence that makes all our business sacred. It transforms our work from something that may be merely secular to a holy partnership with the Lord. Every stroke of work reaches to the uttermost corners of the world.

A little fellow selling newspapers on a city street was being "helped" by his handicapped younger brother. "You would get more done," remarked a gentleman as he bought a paper, "if you did not have your little brother tagging along."

The newsboy looked up as if he had been hit. "What's the use of money if you haven't someone to share it with?" he responded. "I've got Jim to live for, and it helps a lot!"

Sharing. That is what inspires the hand of toil, that is what puts zest into our labor. We are living for Jesus and for a lost world of people who need our Savior. Try taking the Master with you into the workplace. Work for *Him* and for the lost world He loved. You will discover that your job takes on a totally new perspective.

Making good the promise

I see pointed out in this same part of Paul's letter to the Corinthians the carrying out of the commitment that has been made. Paul tells them he has "sent the brethren, lest our boasting of you should be in vain in this behalf; that, as I said, ye may be ready: lest haply if they of Macedonia come with me, and find you unprepared, we (that we say not, ye) should be ashamed in this same confident boasting" (9:3–4). Practical man that he was, Paul knew how easy it was to get sidetracked from a noble goal. How much we need the keeping power of the Holy Spirit and His watchfulness upon our indulgences.

You know the story of the little boy who was given two nickels by his mother, one of which was to be put in the missionary offering at Sunday school. But, as sometimes happens, the boy lost one of them.

"You lost one of your nickels?" exclaimed his mother with mild sympathy. "Now you will have to do without buying any candy."

The boy was unperturbed. "Mother, it was the *missionary* nickel I lost!"

A sharecropper rented some acreage on the agreement that he would keep two-thirds of the produce and give one-third to the owner. When the season passed and the owner had received nothing, he went to the farmer about it. "You were to keep two-thirds of the produce and give one-third to me," he reminded the man.

"That is so," replied the other. "But there were only two thirds. When I came to gather the harvest, I figured there would be three loads, but there were only two!"

Does God get the firstfruits of our earnings, or the leftovers? Do we find the money we want for the special trip or the furniture or the new outfit but short-change God in the process? How much better it is to give systematically and on principle to God.

How much better it is to count the Lord's part first, to "seek . . . first the kingdom of God, and his righteousness" (Matthew 6:33), confident that "all these things [we have need of] shall be added unto [us]."

But what if we cannot pay?

But sometimes, in spite of our best intentions and our most faithful efforts, we cannot meet our commitment. What then? I find in this text great comfort should we be in that circumstance. "If there be first a willing mind, it is accepted according to that a man hath, and not according to that he hath not" (8:12).

An elderly Chinese woman, soundly converted to Christ, had refused to be baptized and finally went to a missionary to discuss the issue. "Why do you not follow your Lord in baptism?" the missionary asked.

"Because I feel I am not worthy to be a disciple of Jesus Christ," the woman replied. "I love Jesus and trust Him, but He tells me in His Book that His disciples must go into all the world and preach the gospel to everyone." She continued, "I can go to my family and to two or three villages near me, and I have done this, but I never can go to all the world."

"Dear sister," the missionary responded, "you do not need to do more than you can do. If the larger willingness is there, God accepts the lesser deed."

God wants our wills and our willingness. If God has withheld the power to make our commitments good after our every honest, earnest and faithful effort, it is no longer our responsibility but His. God will take the will for the deed.

Do not let the failure hang as a millstone around your neck. Leave it behind and start again. Take that great missionary motto set forth by William Carey,

"Attempt great things for God; expect great things from God," and go forth trusting Him. In His strength do your best.

True giving

In summary, true giving to the Lord's causes should have three characteristics. First, it should be in faith. This was the thought in Paul's mind when he said, "God is able to make all grace abound toward you; that ye, always having all sufficiency in all things, may abound to every good work" (9:8). Next, it should be joyful, "for God loveth a cheerful giver" (9:7). And, finally — to return to the text with which we began — it should be inspired by divine love: "Ye know the grace of our Lord Jesus Christ, that, though he was rich, yet for your sakes he became poor, that ye through his poverty might be rich" (8:9).

Freely we have received. May our giving be as generous!